CROCHET

CROCHET

JAMES WALTERS
AND SYLVIA COSH

CONTENTS

First published 1980 by
Octopus Books Limited
59 Grosvenor Street
London W1

© 1980 Octopus Books Limited

ISBN 0 7064 1347 4
D. L.: TO-540-80

Printed in Spain by
Artes Graficas, Toledo

American terms
Although the stitches used in American crochet are identical to those used in Britain, some of them have different names. For example, the British 'double crochet' is the same as the American 'single crochet'. In the stitch instructions that follow, the American term (where it differs from the British one) is given in square brackets. In most of the projects American pattern instructions are given separately to avoid confusion.

HISTORY

Crochet is perhaps the simplest technique for making a fabric. It consists of drawing a series of loops through previously made loops in a continuous thread. The process can be done with the fingers alone; however it is normally done with a hooked pin or stick, which makes the work quicker and more comfortable and permits much finer and more intricate fabrics to be made. The name 'crochet' is derived from the French word *croche*, meaning 'hook'.

The history of the craft is difficult to trace, mainly because the product is perishable but also because the demarcation between one craft and another has not always been as clearly defined as it is today. For example, in some parts of the world hand-knitting was done on needles that had hooks at the end, similar to crochet hooks. Common sense suggests that man would have realized the simple advantages of a hooked tool as a means of manipulating yarn long before he devised the more sophisticated processes and tools used in knitting and weaving. According to tangible evidence, however, weaving of some kind was being practised in the Stone Age; frame-knitting had been flourishing for about 1,000 years when hand-knitting supplanted it at about the time of Christ; and the earliest evidence of crochet dates only from the Middle Ages. Yet we should be wary of taking this apparent order of events literally; the oldest examples of woven and knitted fabrics gives the distinct impression that man had already achieved mastery in all these matters to a degree which defies explanation, long before history began to be recorded. The long and complex period of development before that – the most interesting part of the story – is unlikely ever to be revealed to us now.

The evidence we do have suggests that shepherds and sailors in medieval Europe made rough garments from handspun wool, using bone hooks they would have fashioned themselves. Their method probably resembled that used in Tunisian [Afghan] crochet. This kind of crochet, which uses a long hook and which somewhat resembles knitting, may have evolved from the knitting techniques which had been developed in the Middle East in the pre-Christian era. There is also some evidence that a kind of

Opposite: Made in Ireland during the 19th century, the fine lawn jabot (top) has crocheted ends and an edging of wheel motifs. The very finely crocheted ends consist of circular motifs with one raised flower. The two collars are also examples of Irish crochet. The one above is formed by a very close arrangement of flowers and leaves on a mesh ground with picots. Several of the flowers have raised centres and outlines. The one below consists of sprays of shamrock and flowers powdered on a diamond mesh ground with picots. The scalloped edge is decorated with double loops and the outer one with picots. The early 20th century dress inset (right) is decorated with bold flower motifs.

Right: Early 20th century Irish boudoir jacket. The whole garment is covered with small raised flower motifs. A delicate pink ribbon has been threaded through the neck and hem.

crochet may have been practised in pre-Columbian South America. However, the craft that we now recognize as crochet is the product of a mainly European tradition, which can be traced at least as far back as the Renaissance and which, until recent times, seems to have been entirely decorative rather than practical in character.

Before the 16th century most crochet was simply an alternative procedure for making lace, but gradually it acquired its own distinctiveness. It was usually practised by women in religious orders and was often called 'nuns' lace' or 'nuns' work'. The nuns taught the craft to the daughters of the aristocracy, and it became a popular pastime for ladies, first in Italy and then in Spain and France. When, at the end of the 18th century, the French Revolution caused many noble French families to seek exile, crochet was introduced in the lands where they settled – in Ireland, England and more northerly parts of Europe.

During the 17th century the crochet hook was used for a new kind of embroidery, inspired by Indian work, which became fashionable in Europe. In this technique, called tambour work, the fabric is stretched in a round frame, suggesting a drum (hence the name 'tambour') and chain stitch worked on it with a fine hook. We call this 'surface crochet'. The vogue for tambour work and increasing familiarity with the implement used for it may have helped to stimulate interest in the unsupported kind of crochet – *crochet en air*, as it was called.

Nevertheless, the creative potential of *crochet en air* remained unexplored. It was still considered essentially a technique for making lace, and its practitioners confined their efforts to copying some of the numerous distinctive styles of lace – such as Spanish, Venetian, Renaissance, Honiton, guipure, gros point, filet and reticella – which had been developed through Europe. In Ireland, however, this lace-making tradition produced a quite distinctive and extremely beautiful style. Although still basically a type of fine lacework, Irish crochet has a deep, almost sculptural texture achieved by the ingenious use of padding cords, lumps, bobbles and ridges within the stitch structure itself. The designs, while conforming to certain stylistic guidelines, require a great deal of individual skill and imagination, being compositions of separately made motifs representing natural forms such as flowers, leaves and fruit – each with its own symbolic significance – which are joined by a ground network of delicate chain loops and picots.

It was in Ireland, during the mid-19th century, that crochet – apparently for the first time on any scale – was carried on as an industry. The widespread, acute poverty caused by the potato famine was partially alleviated by the deliberate stimulation of crochet as a cottage industry. The project was initiated, it is said, by the mother superior of the Presentation Convent at Youghal, County Cork, who copied a piece of conventional lace in crochet

and encouraged her nuns to set about teaching people how to do the work in their own cottages. Irish crochet was exported to other countries, notably to England, where it was lavishly used to trim ladies' gowns. Because this form of lace could be made more quickly than others and thus was cheaper, it attracted the epithet 'poor man's lace' – a crushingly inadequate description of this astonishing work.

Crochet became enormously popular in Victorian England, not only for clothing but also for household accessories. The fashions of the times demanded that all surfaces in the home which could conceivably be so adorned (including the legs of furniture) should be smothered with cloths, mats, runners and coverings of all kinds. The speed and ease with which crochet can be accomplished, compared to other needle crafts such as bobbin lace or embroidery, made it well suited to such decorative purposes. After crochet had been featured in the Great Exhibition of 1851 and certain members of the royal family took it up, it became a popular craft among the burgeoning middle classes. Educated ladies with plenty of time and money to spare were keen to learn to crochet.

The resulting demand for instruction and patterns was met by advancing technology in the form of relatively cheap printing methods. Hitherto, crochet techniques and designs had been passed on directly from one person to another. Among the

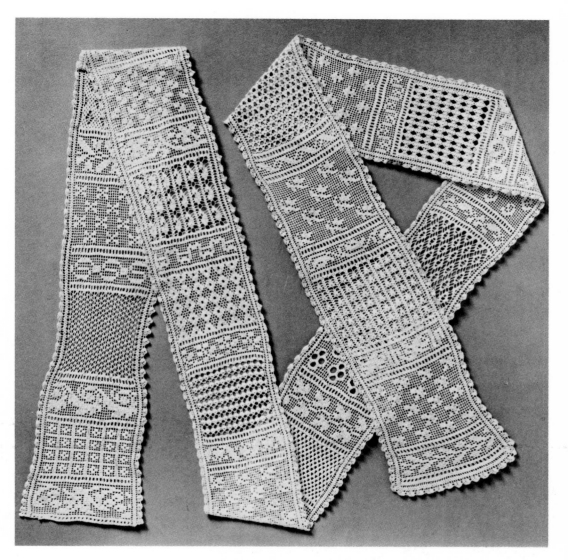

Opposite left: Early 20th century Irish crochet motifs. The motifs were sold ready-made to be assembled with a crocheted ground. Some of the floral sprays are very three-dimensional.

Opposite right: Early 20th century Irish crochet pattern for a lady's collar. Some of the motifs have been completed and placed in position ready to be joined together by a fine mesh background.

Right: English crochet sampler, dated 1837. There are nineteen ground patterns, including both geometric and floral designs.

illiterate majority of the population this method of instruction persisted; bound sets of pattern samples were circulated among communities, each family, if possible, adding a new contribution to the book. However, by the mid-19th century the printed crochet pattern had appeared – thanks largely to the efforts of a gifted Franco-Spanish lady, Mme Riego de la Blanchardière, a refugee from the French Revolution. Mme de la Blanchardière – who had instructed members of the royal family in crochet – collected and organized crochet patterns, devised ways of describing their construction verbally and dispensed this information in print. For some years she ran a monthly magazine called *The Needle*.

By the beginning of the 20th century fashions had changed, and the demand for lace – including the crocheted variety – had subsided dramatically. As a consequence, crochet as an industry died out, and for about 50 years it was rare to find anyone who practised it even as a hobby. Thus the work started by Mme de la Blanchardière and continued by others was of immense importance. Their printed instructions not only introduced the craft to thousands of people who could not have been reached in any other way, but also ensured the survival of a great deal of valuable knowledge, which was later to be rediscovered.

Unfortunately, the long term effects of printed crochet patterns and instructions have not been all good. Written language is

incapable of describing the subtler aspects of a craft; it is forced to ignore them and, by implication, to deny that they exist. This, together with the economic pressures within publishing, has tended to filter out of the crochet pattern market all but the most repetitive and perfunctory designs. Taken as a whole, crochet patterns scarcely suggest the sort of creativity of which the craft is capable. Such, however, is the mesmeric power of the printed word that exaggerated respect is paid to work simply because it has been published, and aspiration towards individual creativity, which is vital to any healthy, living craft, is nipped in the bud.

Something of the versatility of crochet, however, became apparent when it was revived in the 1960s. Instead of duplicating fine lace patterns, as their grandmothers had done, the new generation of crocheters preferred mainly to construct fabrics, similar to those produced by knitting. The long dormant period of the craft has perhaps enabled those taking it up for the first time – particularly young people with no preconceived ideas of it – to approach crochet with fresh eyes. Although one attractive aspect of crochet is the small initial cost involved, its main attraction is probably the immense freedom of expression, which the simple technique encourages. Not only fabrics but also fabric 'painting' and sculpture can be created in this way. In the early 1980s the feeling among practitioners of the craft is that we have only just begun to explore its possibilities.

MATERIALS AND EQUIPMENT

No heavy or expensive equipment is required for crochet. All you need to start is one hook and a few balls of yarn, plus a pair of scissors, a tape measure and a blunt-ended wool [yarn] needle for sewing seams and darning in ends. As you do more crochet you will find many of the following items useful or essential:

1. A range of ordinary and Tunisian [Afghan] hooks; a range of hairpin prongs [an adjustable hairpin lace fork]; a stitch-ripper; a bodkin; rustless pins; a thimble; safety pins and stitch-holders.

2. An iron; a pressing cloth; a selection of padded shapes for pressing three-dimensional work; a teazle wire brush; a ball-winder; a skein-holder; a niddy-noddy for winding yarn into skeins; starch or sugar water.

3. A notebook; a pencil; coloured pens; tag labels for identifying samples and test pieces; graph paper; a pair of compasses [compass]; a protractor; a set square [triangle] and a calculator. (Don't be alarmed by these last few items – mathematics need not enter into crochet at all, except in certain kinds of designing.)

YARNS

The choice of manufactured yarns must be wider today than it has ever been. Among the range of raw materials used are natural ones from animal coats and plant fibres and man-made ones, often in complex blends.

In texture and finish yarns may be soft or hard, matt, lustrous, shiny, glittering, stiff or flexible, smooth, fluffy, hairy, fuzzy, lumpy, loopy or crimped, and they are available in various degrees of thickness. Colour effects include natural and solid monochrome dyed shades, two or more shades plied (twisted together), heather mixtures, marls and space-dyed or 'random' effects.

It takes a lifetime to become familiar with all aspects of these qualities and to be able to express yourself satisfactorily through them, but it is important and rewarding to do so, because the overall effect of anything you crochet will owe at least as much of its character to the yarn you use as to anything you may do with your hook. There are no rules to enable you automatically to select the right yarn for a project; a multitude of practical and aesthetic factors may have to be taken into account. Evaluating them is a personal, individual matter – fortunately – and the best choice may well be instinctive rather than coldly rational. Practical factors that may affect your decision include: machine washability, quickness of drying, durability, weight, comfort in wear, warmth or coolness and vulnerability to moth attack. Natural fibres feel good, look good and hang well but may require more attention than synthetic ones; they may weigh more than synthetics and generally cost more (depending on the changing world economic conditions). Synthetics may be cheaper, lighter and wear better. On the other hand, you may be concerned far more with colour, texture, tactile quality, response to light, or to the yarn's appropriateness to the planned stitch pattern and the general character of the project. Thick yarns will obviously never give you a wispy fabric; intricate patterns will be lost in a highly textured or multicoloured yarn; fine silk, lurex or soft baby wool will contribute little to a practical outdoor garment; clever surface patterning will disappear in a very dark yarn.

You need not confine yourself to knitting and crochet yarns. Plenty of other materials can be used to good effect, particularly in accessories, wall hangings and sculptural work. Raffia, ribbon, leather and suede cut into strips, rope, string and rug and weaving yarns are frequently used; and even such things as bootlaces, straw, fuse wire, acetate and paper in twisted strips, rubber bands and plastic tubing are potential crochet material.

Although the range of materials is enormous, the choice of colours is tending to become more limited. To overcome this limitation, serious crocheters may choose to do their own dyeing, some will even want to do their own hand-spinning.

DYEING

Dyeing need be no more difficult than making a pot of coffee, although when your object is to obtain a precise shade you will need extra skill and patience. For convenience you would probably work with synthetic dyes, which are available in small quantities, already prepared in powder and liquid form to suit most circumstances. Today, however, the growing awareness of the natural environment has led many people to discover the beauty of natural dyes. These come mainly from various parts of plants and trees – from flowers, berries, leaves, twigs, stalks, bark, heartwood and roots.

The dyeing process consists of chopping up and boiling the plant material in water, then immersing the fibres, yarn or fabric in the liquor until it has absorbed the colour. With some species, particularly lichens, that is all you need to do. The majority of plants, however, need the addition of an agent, called a mordant, which fixes the colour. Among the mordants used are alum (potassium aluminium sulphate), chrome (potassium dichromate), tin (stannous chloride), copper (copper sulphate) and iron

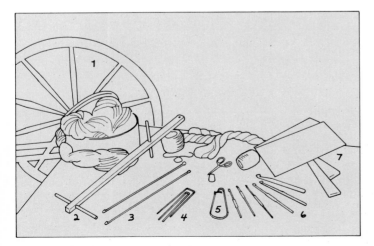

Equipment on pages 10–11
1. spinning wheel; 2. niddy-noddy; 3. Tunisian [Afghan] crochet hooks; 4. hairpin [hairpin lace] crochet prongs [forks]; 5 stitch-holder; 6. ordinary crochet hooks; 7. carders.

(ferrous sulphate). Each mordant has a different effect on the fibres and on the colour obtained: alum usually produces pale shades and leaves the fibres softest; chrome produces bright colours and tin sharp ones; while copper and iron produce dark tones.

Natural dyes yield subtle, glowing colours. Part of the pleasure of using them is observing the varied effects the same kind of plant material can produce. For example, if you treat several skeins of yarn with different mordants, then immerse the skeins in the same dyebath, the result will be a beautifully harmonious range of colours. It is impossible, however, to predict the exact shade that will be produced by any given plant/mordant combination, for this depends upon a host of continuously variable factors, including climate and soil conditions. To confuse matters, there is no relation between the colours of a plant in life and those of the dyes it yields. In general, though, the majority of plants give yellows and/or browns. Grey-greens are also quite common; pinks and purples, rather rare. Clear blues come from indigo and reds from the cochineal beetle and from madder root.

HAND-SPINNING

The great variability of natural materials is a problem for the machine-spinning process, since the main objective is to turn out a completely uniform product. Variations have to be systematically removed and character suppressed by selective breeding and by bleaching and blending. The practical hand-spinner, however, is sensitive and resourceful. He has a different objective – to produce individual yarns in small quantities to suit specific projects – and he works entirely with nature, exploiting the natural beauty of the fibres as they come to him. Beginning with the raw fibre he may sort it, tease it, scour (clean) it, perhaps coax it into a special arrangement or blend it by combing or carding it (stroking it between bats covered with a close pile of angled wire pins). Then he may spin it and ply it (twist together single spun threads) with the aid of a simple spindle or wheel, wind it into skeins, wash it, dry it and wind it into balls. Certainly he will handle it repeatedly and learn to know it intimately.

Some people eventually find complete satisfaction and creative fulfilment from spinning alone. In any event, some acquaintance with these processes is of great advantage to those who crochet. It provides a heightened awareness of the characteristics and performance of different fibres and thread constructions. With this knowledge, even selecting machine-spun yarns becomes as exciting and vital an activity as the work of turning them into fabric.

Apart from the many books available on both spinning and dyeing, the best source of continuing information and advice – if you live in Britain – is your local branch of the Guild of Weavers, Spinners and Dyers. Look out also for adult education classes and workshops and short courses at residential colleges.

HOOKS

Hooks can be made of anything and be of any size. You need a wide range of sizes so as always to be able to make fabrics of suitable density out of any yarn you choose, or to match the tension [gauge] specified in any pattern instructions you may be following. Naturally, mass-produced hooks come in standard sizes. Those conforming to the modern International Standard Range (ISR) have a number stamped on them which is the diameter, in millimetres, of the wide part of the barrel. Older hooks, and those used in the United States, are numbered according to different systems – as shown in the table of comparative hook sizes.

Tunisian [Afghan] hooks are usually longer than ordinary ones and should have a knob at the end. The most convenient hairpin prongs [forks] are rigid and made in a variety of widths, but adjustable ones are also available. A hairpin [fork] is useless if its prongs are pliable.

UK	US
0.60mm	14 steel
0.75mm	12 steel
1.00mm	10 steel
1.25mm	8 steel
1.50mm	7 steel
1.75mm	4 steel
2.00mm	0
2.50mm	B
3.00mm	C
3.50mm	E
4.00mm	F
4.50mm	G
5.00mm	H
5.50mm	H
6.00mm	I
7.00mm	K
8.00mm	11 wood
9.00mm	13 wood
10.00mm	15 wood

BASIC STITCHES

Like every other craft, crochet has its own jargon. It is possible to crochet without knowing any of it, but if you want to follow pattern instructions and learn the techniques described in this book – or to communicate your own designs to others – you will need to familiarize yourself with it. There is no need to memorize all the terms at once; you will gradually pick them up as you go. You may also want to learn the system of symbols which represent the various stitches visually.

ABBREVIATIONS

alt – alternate(ly); approx – approximately; beg – begin(ning); c – contrast shade (also con); cl – cluster; cm – centimetre(s); col – colour; comm – commenc(e)(ing); cont – continu(e)(ing); cr – cross; dec – decreas(e)(ing); foll(s) – follow(s)(ing); gm – gram(s); gr – group; in – inch(es); inc – increas(e)(ing); incl – including; lp – loop; mm – millimetre; M – main shade; patt – pattern; r – raised (prefix to stitches, hence rtr [rdc] = raised treble [double]); rem – remain(ing); rep – repeat; rnd – round; RS – right side of work; sp – space(s); st(s) – stitch(es); st.ch – starting chain; t.ch – turning chain; tog – together; WS – wrong side of work; yrh[yo] – yarn round hook [yarn over] (also yoh, wo, woh, wrh mean the same).

STITCH TABLE

Stitch	Abbreviation	Symbol	American term
chain	ch	⬭	(same)
slip stitch or single crochet	sl st	⌢	slip stitch (only)
double crochet	dc	+	single crochet – sc
half treble	htr	T	half double – hdc
treble	tr	ᵀ	double crochet – dc
double treble	dtr	‡	treble – tr
triple treble	ttr	‡	double treble – dtr
quadruple treble	qd.tr	‡	triple treble – ttr
popcorn	pc	⬭	(same)
puff stitch	p.st	⬭	(same)
raised stitch (treble) at the front	r.tr/f	⌐	raised double at front – r.dc/f
raised stitch (treble) at the back	r.tr/b	⌐	raised double at back – r.dc/b
Solomon's knot	Sk	⬭	(same)
bullion stitch		⫞	(same)
direction of working		⟶	
direction of row		← →	
row number		① ②	
thread markers			
ends of thread			

FIRST ATTEMPTS

Beginners will find it easier to learn stitches using a fairly large hook – say 5.00 mm [size H] – and a smooth, uniform, light-coloured double knitting [knitting worsted] yarn. You will find it useful to practise your first stitches through the edge of an old piece of loosely knitted or woven fabric – anything you can get your hook through. Alternatively, you can work them around a curtain ring or some string tied into a loop.

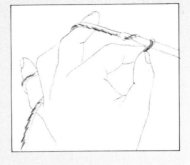

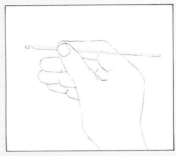

The right hand holds and manipulates the hook, while the left both supports the fabric and controls the supply thread. Exactly how they do their jobs is a personal matter. To begin with you could try to imitate the methods and positions shown here, and allow your own style to evolve naturally through practice.

The first loop

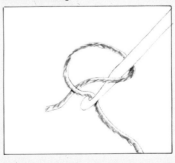
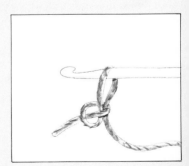

Most crochet starts with a slip knot, which forms the first working loop. (It is the supply thread which slides.)

LEFTHANDED CROCHET

The instructions and illustrations in this book are prepared for righthanded people. Lefthanders work a mirror-image of what is shown and may therefore need a mirror to check the pictures. They should read 'right' for 'left' and vice versa (except in the expressions 'right side' and 'wrong side' of a fabric).

BASIC STITCHES
Chain (ch ⌒)

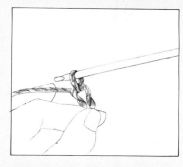

1. Pick up the supply thread by wrapping it round the hook in an anticlockwise direction (lefthanders clockwise); or, if you prefer, manoeuvre the tip of the hook round the yarn. This is called 'yarn round hook' (yrh) [yo].

2. Draw it through the working loop on the hook. One chain stitch has been made and there is a new working loop on the hook.

The slip stitch is exactly the same as the chain, except that you insert the hook through something else first – for the moment, for example, through

your curtain ring or the edge of your old fabric. Unlike free-floating chains, slip stitches become attached to whatever the hook goes through.

3. Make a few chains for practice. To begin with, these may look ugly and uneven and be generally too tight. Do not worry; fluency comes with practice.

Chains and slip stitches have several important functions which you will quickly discover as you make things, but they are of little use in building up a solid fabric.

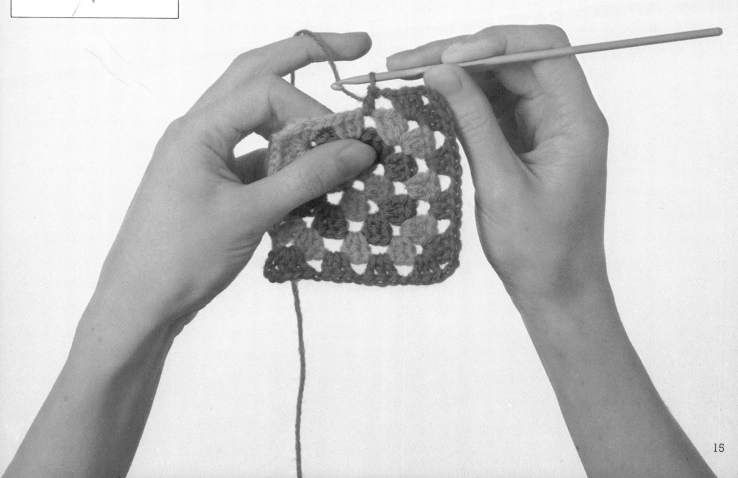

Fabric stitches

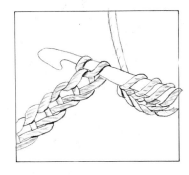

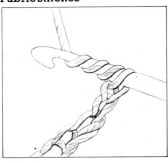

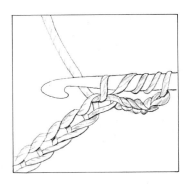

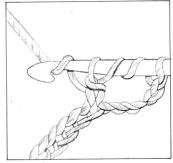

Stitch	Stage 1 yrh [yo]	No. of loops after stage 3	No. of steps in stage 4
double [single] crochet	0	2	1
treble [double]	1	3	2
double treble [treble]	2	4	3
triple treble [double treble]	3	5	4
quadruple treble [triple treble]	4	6	5

There are up to four distinct stages in making a basic stitch:
1. Wrap the yarn round the hook (yrh) [yo] one or more times (this stage may be omitted – see below). In the illustration it has been wrapped three times round the hook.

2. Insert the hook from front to back through some previously made part of the fabric. (In this case the hook has been inserted into one of the initial practice chains. Later on we shall discover all sorts of other places to insert it.)

To begin practising, try working double [single] crochets round the curtain ring or the edge of your old fabric. Note that the yarn is not wrapped at all at the beginning (i.e. stage 1 is omitted), after stage 3 there are only 3 loops left on the hook, there is only 1 step in stage 4 and so the complete stitch is very short and squat. Then move on to the longer stitches. Stitches can be made as long as you like, simply by winding the yarn round the hook as many times as you like; but in conventional crochet, it is unusual to wrap the yarn more than 5 or 6 times.

3. Pick up the supply thread (yrh) [yo] and draw it through the fabric only. (Added to the 3 windings in stage 1 and the original working loop, this makes 5 loops on the hook.)

4. Pick up the supply thread again and draw it through 2 of the loops on the hook, repeatedly, if necessary, until there remains only 1 loop on the hook – the new working loop. The stitch is now complete.

Double [single] crochet

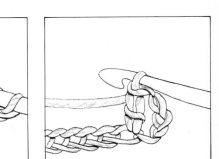

Treble [double] crochet

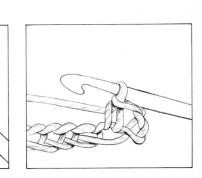

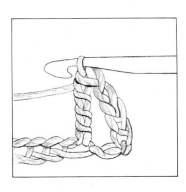

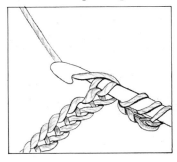

Double treble [treble]

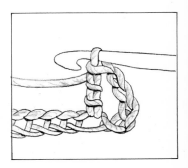

For convenience this procedure is broken down into individual stitches which are defined and named according to how many times the yarn is wrapped at the beginning. Note that the more times this is done, the more loops are left on the hook at the end of stage 3, the more steps have to be taken during stage 4, and the longer (taller) is the resulting stitch.

Triple treble [double treble]

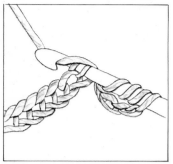
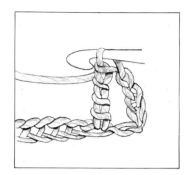

Quadruple treble [triple treble]

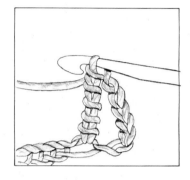

There is one exception to the basic stitch-making procedure described above, and this is the half treble [half double]. For this stitch you work stages 1, 2 and 3 as though you were making a treble [double], so that at the end of stage 3 you have 3 loops on the hook. Then, in stage 4 you wind yrh [yo] and draw the yarn through all 3 loops at once, rather than through 2 and then through the new group of 2, as for a treble [double]. The resulting stitch is, in height, roughly halfway between a double and a treble [a single and a double].

Half treble [half double]

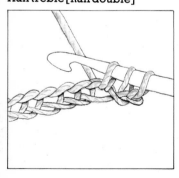
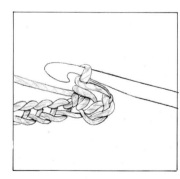

Working in rows

The simplest way of making a solid crochet fabric is to work one row of stitches after another into the top of the previous one. Before you can work the first row it is necessary to have something to put the hook into. This, as we have discovered, could be the edge of some other piece of crocheted, knitted or woven fabric, leather with holes punched into it – or even wooden or ceramic panels – so long as the holes can be made. In pure crochet, however, you usually make a length of chains – called the base or foundation chain – consisting of as many chains as you will want stitches, plus a few more (see instructions for making base chain above).

Base chain

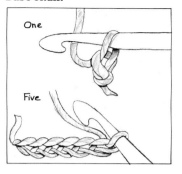
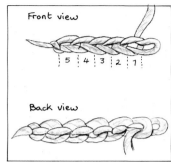

To make a specific number of chains – say 5 – do not count 'one' until you have actually made one; that is, do not count the loop formed by the original slip knot. To check back afterwards on the number you have worked, first make sure you are looking at the front face of the chain length (it easily becomes twisted). Ignore the working loop now on the hook and count the remaining links back to the beginning, including the first which was the original working loop. The very slip knot itself should be tight and small and should not be confused with any of the chains.

If, after much practice and several projects, you find your base chain is always too tight or just difficult to work with, try working with a larger hook, or using 2 strands of yarn together until you begin the first row or making a double chain instead.

Double chain

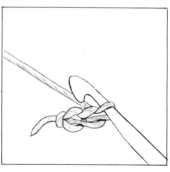
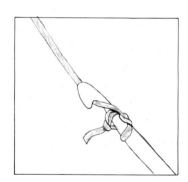
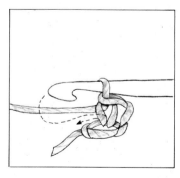
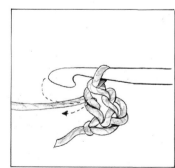

Make 2 ordinary chains. Insert the hook into the first chain made (furthest from the hook) and work 1 double [single] crochet. From now on keep working double [single] crochets by inserting the hook behind the single lefthand vertical thread of the previous double [single] crochet.

ttttttttttttttttttttttt

Tunisian [Afghan] crochet

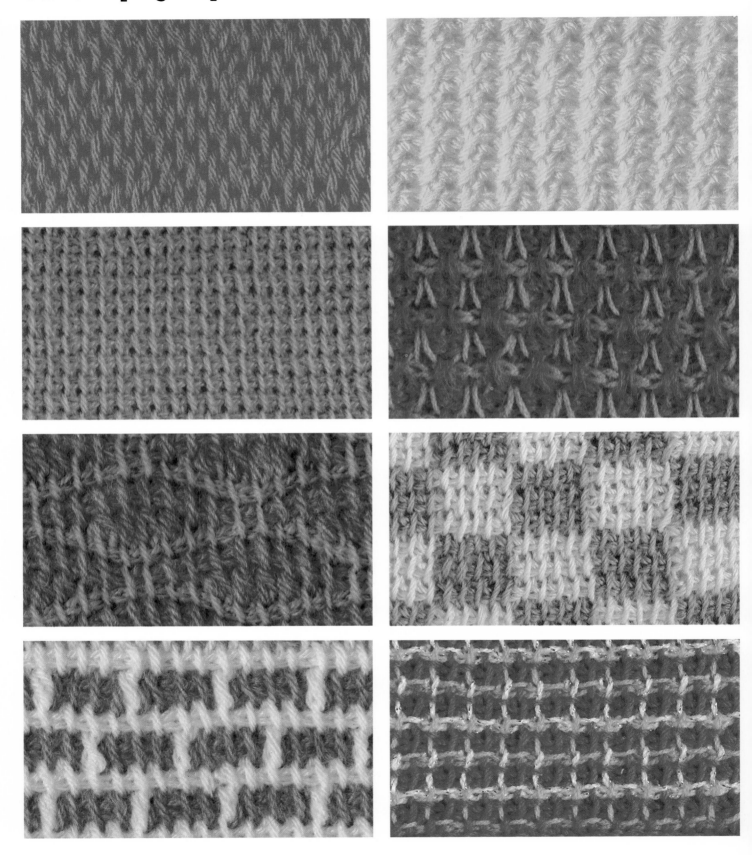

Woven crochet

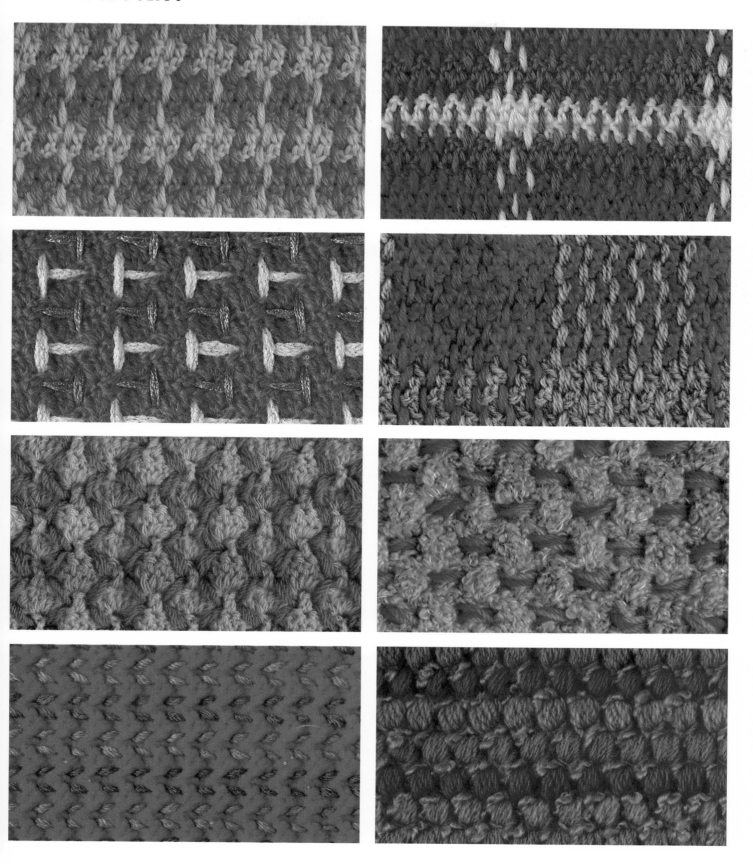

The first row (base or foundation row)

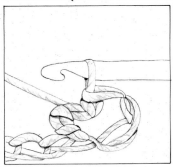

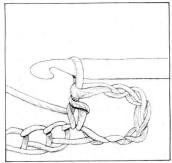

Make a short length of chain – say 6 chains. The next step is to insert the hook into one of the chains you have made, first winding yrh [yo] if the stitch requires it. The question is: into which chain do you insert the hook? This depends upon what stitch you are going to work. If the distance between hook and chain is shorter than the stitch,

then the stitch will not have room in which to stand up; if the distance is longer, then the length of chain will make an unsightly loop and a bad edge to the fabric.

The second row

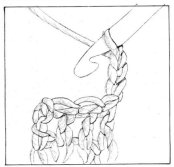

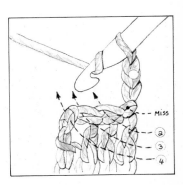

Turning chain: At the beginning of every row after the first you will need to work one or more chains, in order to bring the hook up to the height of the stitch you are intending to work. For dc [sc] work 1 ch, for htr [hdc] 2 ch, for tr [dc] 3 ch, for dtr [tr] 4 ch, and so on. This is called the turning chain (t.ch) and counts as the first stitch in the new row. As you are working in treble [double], make 3 chains.

The stitches of the second and following rows are worked by inserting the hook from front to back under the 2 threads lying on top of each stitch in the previous row (except the first). For special effects the hook may be inserted elsewhere, but in making a plain fabric this is the technique:

Miss [skip] the first stitch and

work 1 tr [1 dc] into the second and third stitches *and into the top of the series of base chains at the end*, inserting the hook under 2 out of the 3 threads making up this top chain. Try and resist the temptation to insert the hook under only *one* thread, or *between* the turning chain and adjacent stitch, or into the next chain down.

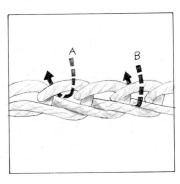

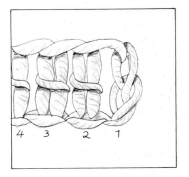

Opinions vary as to the correct number of chains to allow for each stitch, but here is one useful system: for dc and htr [sc and hdc] go into the third chain from the hook (excluding the working loop); for tr [dc] into the fourth, for dtr [tr] into the fifth, for ttr [dtr] into the sixth, and so on. To make a specific number of stitches, therefore, make the base chain that number plus 1 for dc and htr [sc and hdc], 2 for tr [dc], 3 for dtr [tr] and so on. The sample is worked on a base of 6 chains and uses trebles [doubles] (double [single] crochets are much more difficult to see and count); so the first row will include 4 stitches.

Work 1 tr [1 dc] into the fourth chain from the hook (do not count the working loop). It does not matter whether you insert the hook under only the top

single strand or under the top and middle (rear) strands together, so long as you are consistent from one chain to the next. Work another treble [double] into each of the last 2 chains. You have now worked 3 trebles [doubles]. Counting the length of chain at the beginning as the first stitch, you have a total of 4 stitches.

The stitch diagram represents the sample illustrated above it and it is also an exact working model, showing that 6 chains are to be made and 1 treble [double] is to be worked into the 4th, 5th and 6th chains.

Turn the work so that the hook is again on the right.

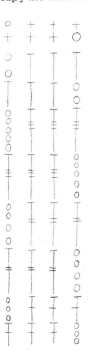

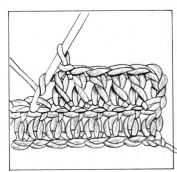

Work several more rows in treble [double] for practice, making sure you always have 4 stitches, including the turning chain, in each row. If you have an extra stitch, the chances are that you have worked into the first stitch in the row by mistake; if you have only 3 stitches, you have probably failed to work into the top of the turning chain in the previous row. When you are reasonably confident working in treble [double], change to double treble [treble] for a few rows, then triple treble [double treble], then back to half treble [half double] and finally double [single] crochet, always maintaining 4 stitches in each row.

Familiarity with the longer stitches, which you can see clearly, helps you to handle double [single] crochet, which tends to be more confusing.

ttr [dtr]   dtr [tr]   tr [dc]   htr [hdc]   dc [sc]

To avoid this darning, if the next row is to be worked with the right side of the fabric facing you (see below), lead both short ends of yarn across the tops of the stitches you are about to work over, and enclose them as you do so. (This method is not suitable on a wrong side row or in openwork stitch patterns.)

If the ball runs out in the middle of a row, drop the old yarn and pick up the new just before you complete a stitch, so that you complete the stitch with the new yarn. If you are working a wrong side row, bring the short ends to the front of the work and keep them under your thumb until you have worked the next stitch. If you are working a right side row, bring them to the back or lay them across the tops of the next stitches so that you can work over them as you continue along the row.

Fastening off

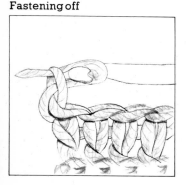

When you have completed a piece of work, cut off the remaining yarn, leaving a tail of about 5cm (2in), work one chain, draw the short end through the last working loop and tighten it gently. This prevents the work from unravelling.

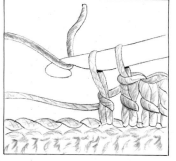

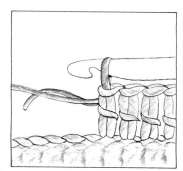

Joining in a new ball

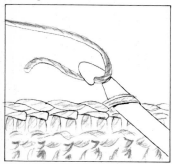

Right side/wrong side

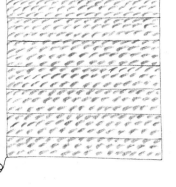

Ideally, you should do this at the end of a row. The simplest method is to fasten off (see above) and proceed as follows: turn the work, insert the hook under the first stitch, drape the new yarn round the hook, draw it through and work the turning chain as usual, keeping your finger on the short end until you have done so. The short ends can be darned in later.

The right side of a fabric is the one which will be on the outside of the completed article and therefore on view. The wrong side is the inside. This almost always matters, even when there does not seem to be much difference between the surfaces. Pattern instructions usually specify your first right side row. When in doubt, consider the right side to be the one uppermost when the beginning length of yarn is at the lower lefthand corner.

DEVELOPING THE TECHNIQUES

SHAPING

When you are confident about keeping the edges of your fabric straight you will be able to add stitches (increase) or eliminate them (decrease) at either or both edges and so change the shape without becoming confused. For convenience the illustrations that follow usually show treble [double] crochet stitches, but the techniques apply to the other stitches also.

To increase more than 2 stitches

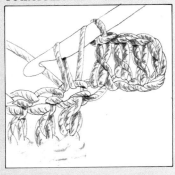
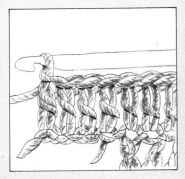

At the beginning of a row: Work a number of chains adding up to one *less* than the number of extra stitches required *plus* the usual turning chain for the kind of stitch you are working. For example, 4 extra stitches in treble [double] as shown need 6 (3 + 3 = 6) chains. Work over these chains as though they were a base chain, i.e. going first into the fourth chain from the hook for trebles [doubles], and continue the row normally.

At the end of a row: Leave your working loop temporarily. Make a separate length of chain with another ball of yarn, making the exact number of chains as extra stitches required – 4 here – and join this with a slip stitch to the top of the edge stitch (turning chain). Fasten off. Return to your working loop and continue over the extra chains.

To increase 1 stitch

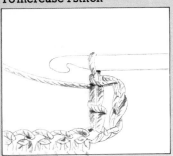

At the beginning of a row: Work the turning chain normally; then, instead of missing [skipping] the first stitch as usual, work a stitch into it.

At the end of a row: Making sure you really have reached the end of a row normally, work a second stitch into the same place as the last (the top of the turning chain).

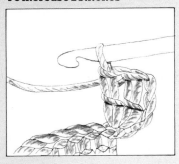

To increase 2 stitches

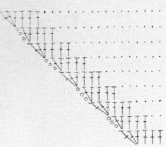

At the beginning of a row, work 2 stitches into the first stitch; at the end, work 3 stitches.

22

A less conventional but quicker way of increasing at the end is to carry on beyond the end in the manner of working double chain, but working stitches one step longer than those you are using for the fabric. Insert the hook behind the single lefthand vertical thread at the base of the previous stitch, complete the stitch in the usual way and repeat for the required number of stitches. For example, if you wanted to make 4 extra stitches in treble [double] you would work 4 double treble [treble] in this way.

At the beginning of a row: Slip stitch across each stitch to be eliminated and into the next one; work the usual turning chain (which will be the new edge stitch) and continue.

At the end of a row: Stop working when you reach the stitches to be eliminated; turn the work and continue as usual. For less sharp steps, work stitches of graduated height.

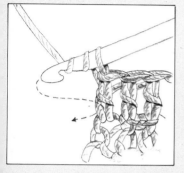 

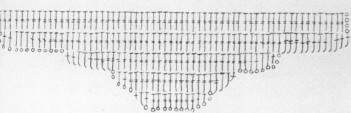

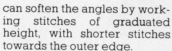

All of these procedures make a sharp step at the edge of your work. If you like – and if your pattern stitch is a long one – you can soften the angles by working stitches of graduated height, with shorter stitches towards the outer edge.

To decrease 1 or 2 stitches

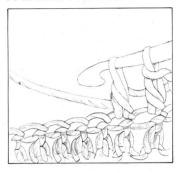 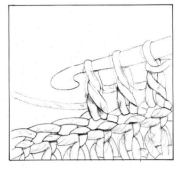

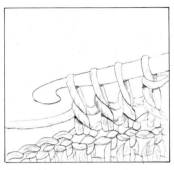 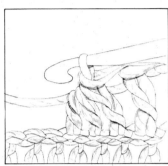

The neatest way to do this – one which prevents a stepped effect at the edges – is to work 2 or 3 stitches together so that they are joined at the top, called a cluster, leaving a single stitch to be worked into on the next row. Each stitch in the group is worked normally up to, but not including, the last step (the final 'yrh' ['yo'] and 'pull through'). After partially working the first stitch you will have 2 loops on the hook (except in htr [hdc] when there will be 3 loops). After the second stitch there will be 3 loops (htr [hdc] 5 loops) and after the third, 4 loops. (It is not practical to try to work 3 htr [hdc] or 3 dc [sc] together.) Complete by winding yrh [yo] and pulling the yarn through all the remaining loops at once.

With fancy, textured and open-work patterns it is obviously not enough merely to increase or decrease; you must also keep in pattern. The best way to determine what you need to do is to study a sample piece of the pattern worked straight. The arrangement and types of stitches used in the pattern will suggest, or even sometimes dictate, ways of increasing or decreasing (below left). In some situations it may be appropriate not to add or subtract stitches at all, but to change periodically to a larger or smaller hook (below right).

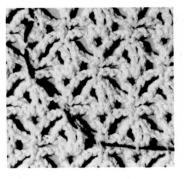 

WORKING IN THE ROUND
Tubes (cylinders)

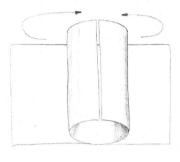 

At the beginning of a row: Work the turning chain normally. (This is counted as the edge stitch as usual.) Miss [skip] the first stitch as usual and work the next 2 or 3 stitches together as described above.

At the end of a row: Work the last 2 or 3 stitches together.
This method of shaping can also be used at other points within a row.
For a more gradual shaping than results from increasing or decreasing one stitch per row, work one or more rows straight (without shaping) between the increase/decrease rows.

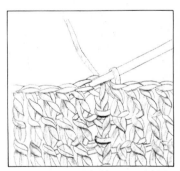 

Imagine a piece of fabric worked in straight rows; now imagine it folded edge to edge and sewn up. You have a tube. In crochet you can make a tube as you go, without having to sew it up afterwards. First join your base chain into a ring with a slip stitch; start each row/round with a turning chain and end it by joining the last stitch to the top of the first stitch (turning chain) with a slip stitch.

You can increase or decrease anywhere you like on the way round to make the tube wider or narrower. Notice that you do not *have* to turn the work at the end of each row/round; you can choose to keep the right side of the fabric towards you at all times; or you can turn it to the wrong side so as to incorporate loops or bobbles, which will then project on the right side.

Circles

Circles are essentially tubes in which the base chain ring is so small as to have almost no space inside it, and the sides, rather than rising up, spread outwards, as a result of constant increasing on each round.

To make a solid flat circle out of any one type of basic stitch, first make 3 or 4 chains and join them into a ring with a slip stitch.

Ovals

To make an oval, first make a length of base chain equivalent to the length of the completed oval *minus* its width.

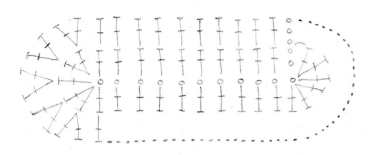

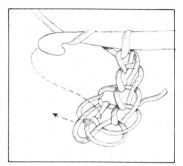 

1st round. Work the usual turning chain – or, as we shall call it in circular work, the starting chain (st.ch) – and count this as the first stitch. Always inserting the hook into the centre of the chain ring – not into individual chains – work a total of 5 or 6 stitches for dc [sc], 8 to 10 for htr [hdc], 12 to 15 for tr [dc], 16 to 20 for dtr [tr] (counting the starting chain as 1 stitch). Join the round with a slip stitch into the top of the starting chain.

2nd round onwards. Always working the starting chain to count as the first stitch and joining up at the end with a slip stitch, add the same number of stitches every round as there are stitches in the first round. This happens automatically if you increase (work 2 stitches into 1) as follows: round 2 – every stitch, round 3 – every second stitch, round 4 – every third stitch, round 5 – every fourth stitch, and so on, working 1 stitch per stitch between the increases.

1st round. Work along the base chain as you would if working in rows. Into the last chain work enough extra stitches to make a semicircular fan shape, bringing the hook round to the unworked side of the base chain. Continue working stitches into the chains, and at the other end work a number of stitches into the last chain, making a fan shape as before. Join the last stitch to the starting chain with a slip stitch.

2nd round onwards. Work in the same manner as for a circle, but increase only over the curved sections of each round. If you spread the necessary increasing equally round the whole circumference, the shape will become more circular with every round worked. If you restrict it to within the curved ends, the shape will continue to be elongated.

Spirals

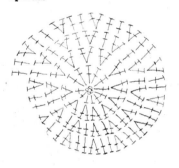 

If you would rather not have to cope with numbers, you can work by common sense and 'feel', like this:

2nd round onwards. Work 1 stitch into every stitch until your last stitch seems to be leaning back (to the right) far enough for you to be able to work another in the same place without this one leaning forward (to the left) too much. (In round 2 this should happen with every stitch.) Check the work frequently by putting it down on a flat surface and making sure that it is neither forming ripples through too much increasing, nor curling up round the edges through too little. Good judgement comes with practice.

Another way of working in the round (to make tubes, circles or ovals) is in a continuous spiral, rather than in separate joined rounds. It is useful, nevertheless, to mark the beginning of each round with a contrasting thread. This method is sometimes more popular with beginners, but it is less flexible: you cannot change your mind while working as to which side of the work you want facing you, and you cannot make closed bands of colour by changing the yarn. To end without a 'step', gradually reduce the height of stitches.

1st round. Work as many stitches into the ring as seem adequate and comfortable. Too many is better than too few.

Other shapes worked in rounds

Not only circular shapes are made in the round. Squares – including the granny square – and shapes with 6 or more sides are quite common, particularly in patchwork crochet; pentagons and triangles, though equally feasible, are less popular. Shapes may be abstract patterns or represent flowers and leaves etc.

ROW SHAPES

So far we have considered only simple row shapes. The process of increasing and decreasing can be used not only to shape the overall fabric but also to make interesting shapes out of the rows themselves. The technique of using different heights – normally associated with increasing texture – also plays a part here.

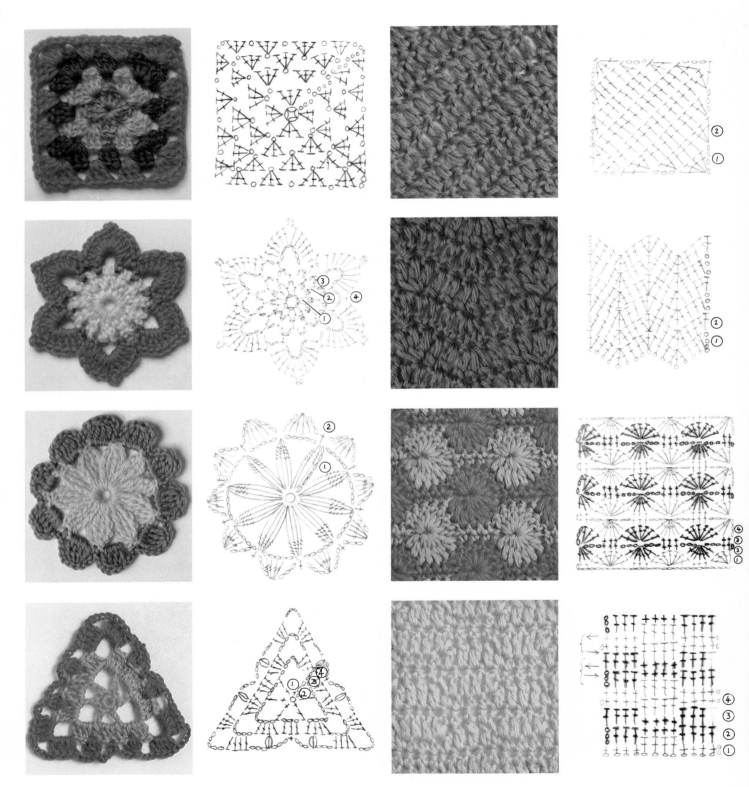

TEXTURE

Crochet is capable of producing fabrics with many interesting surface textures. Here are some of the techniques:

1. Work into the back loop only of each stitch (dc) [sc].
2. Work stitches of different lengths (normally) alternately (dc/dtr) [sc/tr].

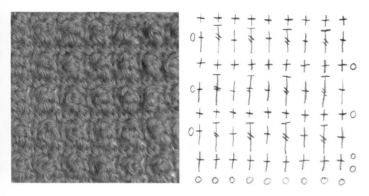

3. To work a raised stitch (round the stem), insert the hook from right to left in and out again behind the stem, either at the front or at the back of the fabric.

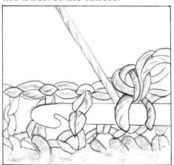 

 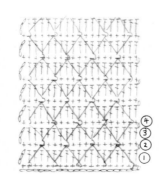

4. Popcorn 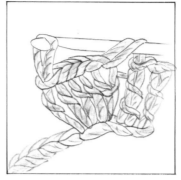 Work a group of stitches into the same place. Remove the hook from the working loop, insert it through the top of the first stitch in the group, pick up the working loop again and pull this through to close up the top of the group and push it out on the right side of the fabric.

5. Puff stitch  *Yrh [yo], insert hook, yrh [yo], pull loop through fabric and up to height of treble [double], rep from * 4 or 5 times all into the same place, yrh [yo], pull through all except the last loop, yrh [yo], pull through last 2 loops.

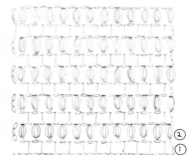

27

6. Bobble (Work on wrong side rows.) Work 5 tr [dc] all into 1 stitch, but omit the last step each time, as for working stitches together – 6 loops on hook – yrh [yo], pull through all except last loop, yrh [yo], pull through last 2 loops.

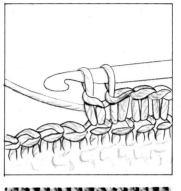
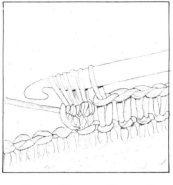

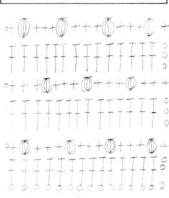

7. Bullion stitch Yrh [yo] 10 times, insert hook, yrh [yo], pull through fabric, yrh [yo], pull through all loops (pick each loop off the hook individually if necessary). Work 1 ch to complete.

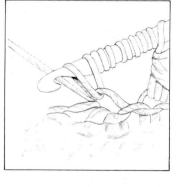
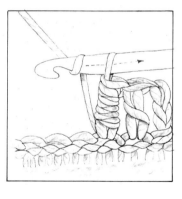

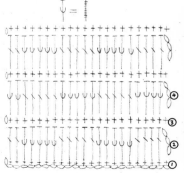

8. Loop stitch (Work on wrong side rows.) Insert hook and extend (middle) finger to form loop, take hook over and to the right of the thread between work and finger, pick up the supply thread between finger and ball. Pull back and through fabric – 2 loops on hook. Go to the left of the loop threads, pick up supply thread and pull through both loops to complete. Remove loop from finger.

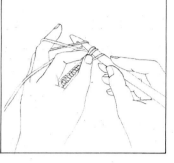
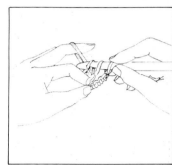

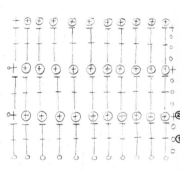

9. Spike Insert hook through fabric from front to back in desired position, yrh [yo], pull through and up to height of current row *loosely*, insert hook in next stitch normally, yrh [yo], pull through fabric – 3 loops on hook. Yrh [yo], pull through all loops.

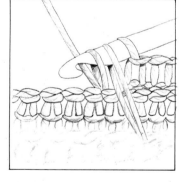
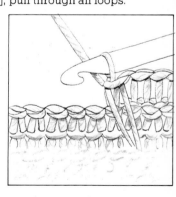

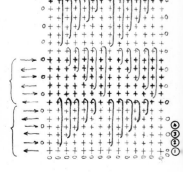

OPENWORK

Perhaps the most characteristic patterns in traditional crochet are openwork. Some of the main elements in these patterns are chain spaces, groups, clusters and crossed stitches. A 'group' is an arrangement of complete stitches all worked into the same place. A 'cluster' is the opposite: several stitches often started in different places but all joined together into one at the top.

Filet crochet is a regular network or grid in which patterns or even pictures are made by filling in some of the spaces with trebles [doubles].

Filet

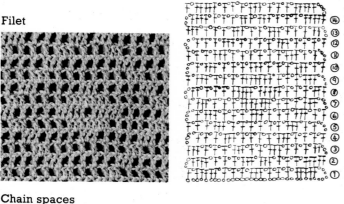

Chain spaces

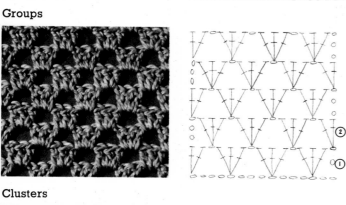

Groups

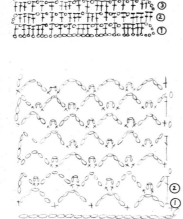

Clusters

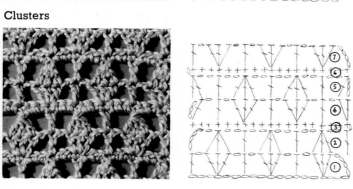

Solomon's knots

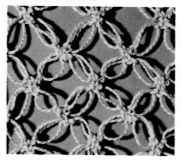

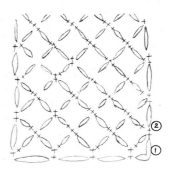

Pineapples

Crossed stitches

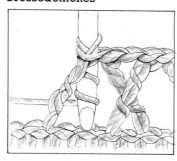

To cross a pair of stitches and make an 'x' shape, miss one or more stitches and work the first stitch into the next, then, if you have missed more than 1 stitch, work a chain or chains (1 less than the number of missed stitches). Work the second stitch into the first missed stitch – bringing the hook *behind* the first stitch, then working it into the front of the fabric as usual.

Solomon's knots

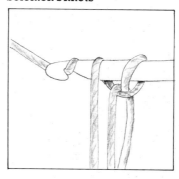

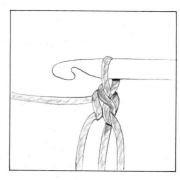

Begin by making a slip knot, plus 1 ch; pull up the working loop to the length required (this will determine the distance between knots); 1 ch, insert hook in back thread of long chain, make 1 dc [sc], i.e. yrh [yo] and pull loop through – 2 loops on hook – yrh [yo] and pull through both loops. One

Solomon's knot has been made. To make the classic network illustrated, make the knots which are drawn more heavily approximately half as long again as the rest. At the junctions in the network, work the dc.s [sc.s] into the centres of the dc.s [sc.s] between chain loops.

SURFACE CROCHET

Surface crochet is a way of adding bulk and firmness to a fabric or simply of embellishing it afterwards.

The simplest approach is to take some previously made plain fabric and apply stripes or other patterning to it, or to draw your own picture. The most successful surface crochet, however, is done on a planned background fabric, where the surface work is part of a well integrated design.

1st method (surface slip stitch). This method creates a shallow relief pattern. Holding the fabric flat and always retaining the supply thread underneath (on the wrong side), insert the hook down through the fabric from the right side. Make the usual slip knot and draw this through (hold the knot itself in place underneath with your other hand). * Insert the hook down through the fabric again in another place, yrh [yo] (underneath), draw the yarn through both the fabric and the loop on the hook. Rep from *, inserting the hook at points chosen so as to form the line you wish to 'draw' on the fabric. Turn the fabric or the hook in order to change direction.

2nd method. In this method both the supply yarn and hook are kept above the fabric. Support the fabric in any way that seems convenient at the moment, and crochet normally, inserting the hook wherever and however you need in order to build up the desired effect. With the first method it is much easier to see what you are doing and where you are going, but there is a limit to the depth and textural interest you can achieve. A combination of both methods may be appropriate in some cases. With either method be careful not to work too tightly or otherwise to distort the background fabric.

TUNISIAN [AFGHAN] CROCHET

For Tunisian crochet you need a special hook – longer than the ordinary kind and with a knob at the end. Rows are worked in pairs; the first, which is worked from right to left, consists of making new stitches by picking up loops and retaining them on the hook; the second consists of casting [binding] these off as the hook returns towards the righthand edge of the fabric.

Tunisian crochet produces a firm fabric, particularly suitable for blankets, cushion covers and outer garments. The basic technique can be varied to include additional colours and to create different textures and even openwork.

Basic technique

Base chain. Make the same number of chains as stitches required.

1st row (outward). Insert the hook into the 2nd chain from the hook, * yrh [yo], draw loop through * – 2 loops on hook; rep from * to * into each chain, retaining all the new loops on the hook; do not turn.

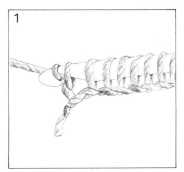

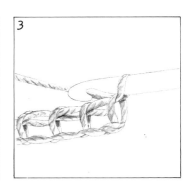

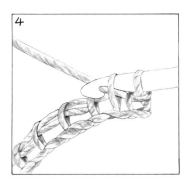

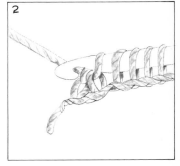

2nd row (inward). Yrh [yo], draw through 1 loop, * yrh [yo], draw through 2 loops; rep from * until there is only 1 loop left on the hook and the hook is back at the righthand edge of the fabric; do not turn.

3rd row (outward). Count the loop on the hook as the first stitch; then, beginning at the 2nd stitch of the previous row and always inserting the hook from right to left behind the single vertical thread at the front of each stitch, work across the row, picking up new loops in the same way as for 1st row. Check that you have the correct number of loops on the hook before you begin the next row. It is very easy to miss [skip] the last stitch on the outward row.

4th row (inward). As 2nd row.
Repeat 3rd and 4th rows.

HAIRPIN [HAIRPIN LACE] CROCHET

Hairpin crochet is worked with an ordinary crochet hook on a special prong [fork] or frame [loom] of thin parallel steel pins. The procedure is to make a number of separate strips of hairpin fabric and then join these into larger pieces or whole garments. A strip can be any length, but its width depends upon the width of the prong [fork]. These are available in various widths, or you can buy an adjustable prong [fork]. The character of hairpin work is usually light, open and delicate.

Basic technique. First make a slip knot in your yarn. Hold the prong [fork] with the points upwards, drop the loop over the righthand pin and draw it out until the knot is midway between the pins. Revolve the prong [fork] half a turn (clockwise, as viewed from above). Control the supply thread with the left hand and hold the hook in the right, as usual, while supporting and manipulating the prong [fork] with both hands. Insert the hook into slip loop; yrh [yo], pull loop through; * with the last loop still on the hook, take the handle of the hook over and behind the righthand pin. Revolve the prong [fork] half a turn clockwise. Insert the hook under the front thread of the last loop made on the lefthand pin, i.e. to the left of the central spine. Work 1 dc [sc]. Repeat from *.

Patterns usually consist of making a specific number of loops round each pin. Check that you have the same number on each side. To make a long strip on a short prong [fork], remove all the loops periodically and replace the last 2 or 3 on each side. Fasten off in the usual way. The construction of the central spine of stitches can be varied, but the main effects in hairpin crochet are achieved by the ways in which the strips are joined.

Joining the strips

When the strips are released from the prong [fork] the loops tend to twist. Be sure to decide whether you want them twisted or not in the finished result and work accordingly.

Simple join (requires no extra yarn). Place the strips to be joined side by side. Pick up the 1st loop of the 1st strip, then the 1st loop of the 2nd strip; pull this through the 1st loop of the 1st strip. Pick up the 2nd loop of the 1st strip; pull this through the loop on the hook. Pick up the 2nd loop of the 2nd strip; pull this through the loop on the hook. Continue up the strips, finally sewing the last loop firmly in place to prevent unravelling.

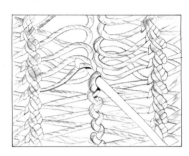

Slip stitch join (requires an extra ball of yarn). Make a slip loop in the extra yarn on the hook. Holding the supply thread at the back of the work * insert the hook into the 1st loop of the 1st strip and into the 1st loop of the 2nd strip; make lss; rep from * into each pair of loops. Fasten off as usual.

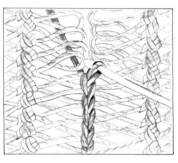

WOVEN CROCHET

Almost any crochet fabric can be woven afterwards, but conventionally the technique is most often used to transform horizontal stripes, worked perhaps in plain trebles [doubles] or filet mesh, into interesting checks and plaids. A fabric which has been well woven is much firmer and thicker than before and becomes suitable for cushion covers, outer garments and bags.

The technique

Use a blunt-ended wool [yarn] needle with a large eye. Do the weaving with the right side of the fabric facing you and before you sew up any seams. Patterns may call for one or more double strands of yarn to be woven horizontally, vertically, diagonally or in zigzag formation. Try to thread your needle with enough yarn to work one or more complete rows, because there is no way to join yarn satisfactorily in the middle. Work with a darning action, passing the tip of the needle cleanly over and under the background stitches without splitting threads. Beware of

shrinking or distorting the background fabric by drawing the woven strands too tight. To finish, knot the ends of the woven strands into a fringe; or darn them into the wrong side of the fabric as neatly as possible.

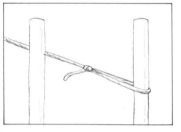
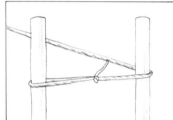
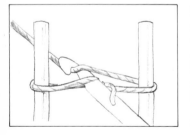
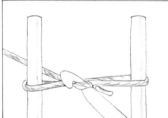
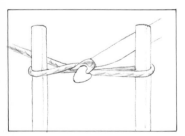
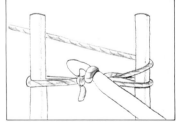
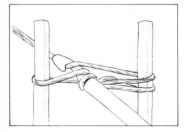
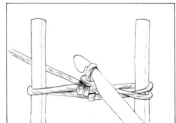

SETTING TO WORK

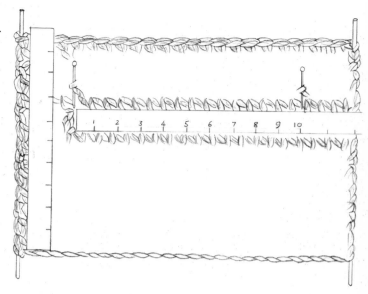

Once you have learned the basic crochet techniques, you can make things. There are 2 ways of doing this: either buy a published pattern or devise something original. Most people are far too lacking in confidence to try the second alternative, which is a pity. An original design does not have to be complicated; it may well be more difficult to reproduce someone else's design. On the other hand, some people are so put off by the language of conventional instructions, or by the designs available, that they can only work on their own. This is also a pity, for they are missing a certain amount of valuable (and almost free) instruction and experience.

The projects in this book are designed to help you learn to follow a pattern and also to make your own designs. Try not to regard them as final and fixed in every detail, but as bases for your own adaptations and sources of ideas, which you can reinterpret and transform into original work.

One piece of advice for the absolute beginner: for your first project, select something in which the final shape and size are not of crucial importance. Later, when you have learned to work smoothly, with an even tension [gauge], you can advance to projects requiring precise measurements.

FOLLOWING CONVENTIONAL PATTERN INSTRUCTIONS
On the face of it you have nothing to worry about, once you have chosen your pattern. The amount and type of yarn you will need is specified, a hook size is suggested and all the details of the pattern and its individual pieces are provided. What can go wrong? The answer is, quite a few things; but fortunately, with a little care and attention, mistakes can be averted – or at least remedied before they cause big problems. Here are some of the potential problem areas:

Yarn
If you cannot obtain the yarn specified and do not know what it is like, it is inadvisable to proceed with a substitute without redesigning the whole project from scratch – that is, working out the stitches and rows required for the measurements given. Even if you are familiar with the designated yarn, substituting a similar yarn can be risky.

Tension [gauge]
At the beginning of the instructions the designer states the number of stitches, and sometimes also rows, obtained over a given measure – usually 10 cm (4 in). It is from this that all the calculations are made. *The article you make will only be the size you intend if your tension is the same.* Even having the correct yarn and using the suggested hook size will not automatically guarantee this, because tension varies enormously from one person to another. However experienced you are, the only way to find out if your tension is the same is to make a test specimen of the pattern with the appropriate yarn, starting with the suggested hook. Make the specimen at least half as wide again as the required measure – i.e. 15 cm (6 in) instead of 10 cm (4 in). One or 2 rows are not enough; continue working until your piece is square. Without pulling it about, place it on a flat surface and slip in a couple of pins to bracket the number of stitches specified for the given measure. Do not include either side edge inside the portion to be measured, because the stitches there are unrepresentative of overall tension. Then measure the distance between the pins. If the pins fall inside the set measure your tension is too tight. Make another test piece using a size larger hook. If the pins fall outside

the measure, try again with a size smaller hook. Also check the row tension in the same manner, if this is specified in the pattern.

If you can't get the tension right, irrespective of the hook – for example, if the stitch tension is correct but the row tension is not – this does not mean you are unusual or incompetent. You may need to make some alterations in the pattern instructions, based on your own tension, for instance, the number of stitches and/or rows required.

By the time you have finished one or more test specimens you will also have sorted out and probably memorized the stitch pattern. In the case of complicated patterns this gives you a good 'running jump' on the project itself – so the tension square can be useful in more ways than one. (Don't throw it away; it might serve as a pocket, or as a piece of patchwork.)

Measurements
When instructions for several sizes of garment are included, figures for the smallest size are given first, followed by those for the larger sizes in parentheses. When only one set of figures is given, this refers to all sizes.

Diagrams, symbols and charts
Stitch symbol diagrams and charts are pictorial representations of the crochet work as it will appear when you construct it. Charts show the right side of the fabric, and so you must remember – when the method of working involves turning at the ends of the rows – to read every second row from left to right. In Fair Isle or jacquard charts each space represents one stitch (usually double [single] crochet unless otherwise stated). In filet charts the squared lines represent the basic grid of trebles [doubles] and chain spaces. Where squares are filled in or cross-hatched you must similarly fill in those squares by working trebles [doubles] instead of the chain spaces.

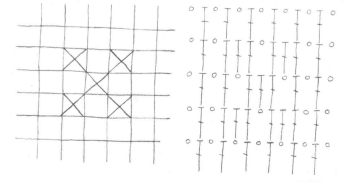

Abbreviations and terminology

It pays to become familiar with the terms and abbreviations listed in Chapter 3, because they are used extensively throughout the project instructions, as well as in pattern leaflets. Any special procedures called for in a project but not explained on the spot will be found in the relevant chapter. When the word 'repeat' (rep) occurs in conjunction with an asterisk, repeat the sequence of stitches following the asterisk as many times as necessary to reach the end of the row, or to within the last few stitches, if so instructed. If the instruction reads, 'rep from * 10 times', this means work the sequence 11 times altogether, because you have already worked it once before the repetition starts. If a sequence is enclosed in parentheses, e.g. '(1 tr, 1 ch, 1 tr) 10 times', the stitches within the parentheses should be worked the exact number of times specified.

Once you have established the correct tension [gauge] and stitch pattern, you are half way to producing a successful article. Study the text slowly, carefully and in sequence, particularly where repetitions are indicated. Misreading the occasional word or even the position of a comma may make nonsense of the instructions.

If your base chain has to be very long you cannot ever be quite sure you have worked exactly the right number. To be safe, try to work more than enough, or leave a generous tail of spare yarn when you make the initial slip knot and use this to work a few extra chains later if necessary. A few unwanted chains can easily be unravelled before you make up the article.

Develop the habit of frequently checking details, such as the number of stitches or pattern repeats, as well as the overall appearance of the work; hold it out at arm's length occasionally and have a good look at it. The important points for making a careful check are: (1) after the base row; (2) after the first pattern row; (3) after the first complete pattern sequence; (4) just before beginning, while working and after completing a sequence of shaping. Whenever you discover that you have made a mistake, resist the natural impulse to unravel the work immediately. Leave it until you are quite sure what went wrong; otherwise you may easily repeat the mistake.

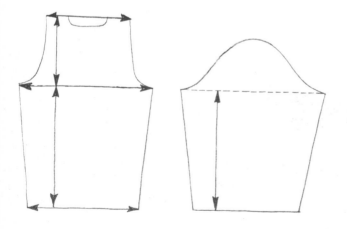

When you check the dimensions of a piece of fabric against the instructions, always place it on a flat surface and align your tape measure or straight edge exactly with the rows (for width) or at right angles to the rows (for length/depth). Never try to measure the depth of an armhole, for example, or a shaped side by running the tape around the edges. Finally, however impatient you may feel to complete a project, do not rush or cut corners during the final making up. Haste at this point can utterly ruin hours of good, painstaking work.

DOING IT YOURSELF

There are two main approaches to designing your own crochet: conventional and free. The conventional way is to make designs more or less like those in published patterns. To begin with you might make adaptations of existing patterns. Apart from deciding on the article, you must select the yarn and stitch pattern, work out the most appropriate method of construction, make a tension [gauge] specimen, calculate from this the numbers of stitches and rows you need at various points to make the pieces to the right measurements and plan the shaping details.

Although it sounds complicated, this process is very satisfying, because at each stage you are expressing your own tastes and capabilities. You will obviously not choose a yarn you cannot obtain, nor a stitch pattern or shaping you cannot easily manage. You could even include pieces of leather or woven fabric. You may have to make a number of sample squares before you are satisfied with the feel and look of the tension [gauge], but the end result will be a reflection of your own decision, rather than an imitation of someone else's results. There is a guide to what size hook to try with different yarns in Chapter 2. To make a very stiff fabric, choose the smallest hook you can possibly work the yarn with; otherwise pick the most comfortable one. With an uneven yarn, suit the hook to the thickest part.

Your main technical problems, apart from the arithmetic, are likely to be deciding what size and shape to make the piece or pieces and estimating how much yarn to buy. Unfortunately, there is no way round a little arithmetic, but a cheap pocket calculator will make short work of it. Learn about pattern pieces both by studying other designers' patterns (crochet, knitting or dressmaking) and by analyzing your favourite garments. Before you can estimate your yarn requirements you must buy one or two balls of your chosen yarn and work a large sample to your chosen stitch pattern and tension [gauge]. By comparing the area of crochet produced with this yarn and the total area of crochet required for the article, you can figure the number of balls you will need altogether. A potential problem is that when you visit the supplier the second time, to buy the remaining yarn, no more yarn of that dyelot – or even that quality – may be available. Thus, the conventional approach can actually be costly in money as well as in time.

The free approach can be more practical in this respect, and more fun. If your fabric need not conform to a rigid grid of regular rows and uniform repeat patterns in a single shade or texture over large areas, you can sit down with a heap of assorted yarns and build up a fabric as you go along. You can add bits here, there and everywhere in all directions without a thought for numbers or whether you will run out of a particular yarn.

If the fabric must be a precise size, you can work to an outline of the piece(s), (either your own drawing or a paper pattern piece). As you crochet, you are, in effect, filling in this shape, as you might fill in an outline shape when doodling on a telephone message pad. It is a small step from purely random fabric building of this kind to working round preconceived design elements – colour schemes, textures, geometrical or organic pattern shapes and representational features, such as trees, flowers, or even whole landscapes.

One way of filling in a shape is to make a number of small pieces and join them together later. You can work some in rounds or spirals, some in undulating or curved rows. The pieces can be joined by crochet or by sewing, in whatever way seems appropriate – first, perhaps, into several small areas and then into larger ones.

Obviously this kind of designing is very much a matter of trial and error – but with many successes and happy surprises along the way. Don't expect to be right the first time every time; be prepared to try different approaches and even to modify your original intentions as experience dictates. Have fun!

FINISHING

Darning in ends

If you need to dispose of stray ends of yarn, darn them neatly into the wrong side of the fabric with a blunt-ended wool [yarn] needle.

Pressing and blocking

Information about how to treat each yarn is printed on the ball band of branded yarns. Ignore this at your peril! Pressing some yarns can be quite fatal, and it is generally not recommended for crocheted fabrics, particularly those with raised textures or relief designs. With flat cotton lacework, however, pressing may be essential. In the absence of manufacturer's instructions, press cotton with a hot iron, wool and mohair (if you must) with a warm one and nylon with a cool one. Use a damp cloth for cotton, wool and mohair and a dry one for nylon. You need to use firm pressure on cotton, light to firm on wool, light on nylon and very light (just touching the pressing cloth so as to steam) on mohair. Do not press acrylic or glitter yarns at all.

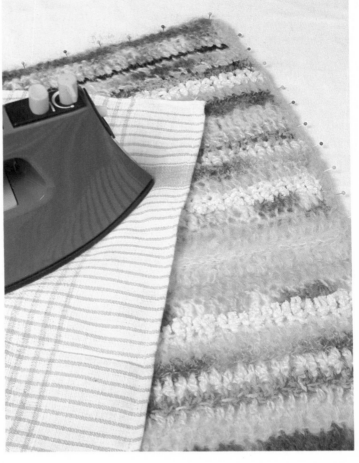

To press a piece of crochet, lay it wrong side uppermost on a well-padded surface. A blanket over a few layers of newspaper on the kitchen table is usually more convenient than an ironing board. Gently pat the fabric into the correct shape and pin it along the edges, using pins liberally, until the rows and edges are straight. Lay the pressing cloth on top of it. Apply the iron by lifting it up and down – never run it to and fro. Leave the fabric pinned in position until it is completely cool and dry.

Seams and joining

Pattern instructions generally tell you in what order to join seams but do not specify the method. Seams may be joined in several ways, using either sewing or crochet, as shown in the illustrations. Backstitch (1) makes the strongest seam, but a bulky one. A flat seam (2) (essentially a close running stitch) is useful where an inconspicuous join is important. Use slip stitch [sewing] (3) for attaching surface features and herringbone [catchstitch] (4) for setting elastic into waistbands. Take care to align rows at side seams and not to distort the fabric by sewing too tightly. Use the garment yarn itself for sewing, unless it is too thick or uneven.

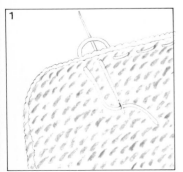
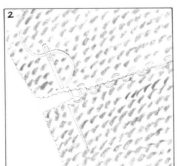
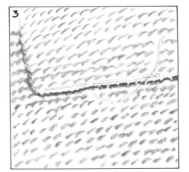
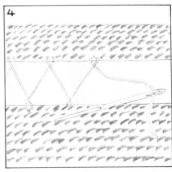

Crochet joins. Edges may be joined by working slip stitch or double [single] crochet through both thicknesses together. These techniques are generally used as an alternative to a backstitch seam. A double [single] crochet seam, which produces a pronounced ridge, can be used as a visible design feature. For this purpose the two pieces of fabric are placed with their wrong sides together.

Edgings

Most crochet fabrics need to have their edges made neater and firmer through the addition of some kind of edging. The simplest edging is a single row of double [single] crochet, worked with the right side facing. It is important to achieve consistent tension [gauge] and to distribute the stitches evenly and at intervals so that there is no distortion of the fabric. There are no easy rules to guide you in this process; be prepared to unravel and try again.

 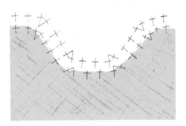

When more than one row of edging has to be worked, it is important to increase and decrease round corners and curves to keep the work flat and the shape true. As a guide, in going round a corner or curve of 90 degrees in double [single] crochet, increase or decrease 2 stitches every row. For a sharp corner work these in the same place, but spread them for a gradual curve.

Picot edging. For a pretty, delicate edge picots are appropriate. There are several kinds of picot edging. Here is a simple one: Work 1 row dc [sc], making sure you have an odd number of stitches; work 1 dc [sc] to count as 1st dc [sc] of picot row; miss [skip] 1st dc [sc]; * 1 dc [sc] into next dc [sc], 3 ch, sl st into 1st ch to form picot, 1 dc [sc] into next dc [sc]; rep from * to end.

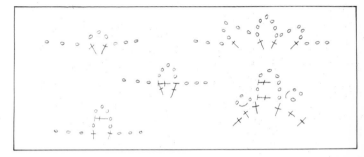

Corded edge. After working 1 row of double [single] crochet, with the right side facing, do not turn but work another row of dc [sc], this time working from left to right as follows: * insert hook in next stitch to the right, yrh [yo], pull loop through fabric but not through loop on hook, yrh [yo], as though you were going to the left again normally, pull through 2 loops; rep from * to end.

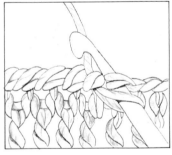 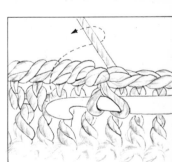

Buttons

Simple buttons can be made by working 2 or 3 rounds in double [single] crochet as for a flat circle, followed by 1 round without increasing and then 2 or 3 decreasing. Before the hole becomes too small, pack the crochet with stuffing or spare yarn. Fasten off, leaving sufficient thread to close the hole and sew on the button.

Buttonholes

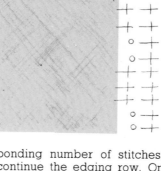

Simple buttonholes can be made during edging rows, as follows:
Work 2 or 3 chains, depending on the size of button required, and miss [skip] a corres- ponding number of stitches; continue the edging row. On the next row, if any, work at least as many stitches into the buttonhole loop as there are chains.

Fringe

To make strands for fringe, wind the yarn round a book or a piece of sturdy cardboard

about 20 per cent wider than the depth of fringe required. Cut through the yarn at 1 edge. Take as many strands as required, fold them in half and knot them through the main fabric. For a knotted fringe you must, of course, cut longer strands. After tying them to the fabric as described above, separate the bundles of strands and tie half of each bundle to half of the adjacent bundle on each side. Work over a ruler to ensure consistent depth of knots. Work more than 1 row of knots in this way if you like.

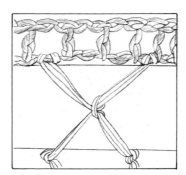

Twisted cord

Cut strands of yarn 3 times the finished length of the cord. (The number of strands will vary according to the yarn and the project.) Tie the strands together at each end and insert a pencil in each knot. Get someone to help you twist the yarn. While always keeping the strands taut, each person should turn the pencil clock-wise, or in the same direction as the twist in the yarn, until the yarn is *very* tightly twisted – on the point of kinking. Without relaxing the strands, fold in half to bring the already knotted ends together. Release the

folded end and give the cord a sharp shake, then smooth it along its length. Make another knot at each end. Trim both ends to make tassels.

Curlicue

Make a length of chain as long as the curlicue required; then, starting into the third chain from the hook, work 5 trebles [double crochets] into every chain. Fasten off, leaving suf- ficient thread to sew on the curlicue. The spiral effect hap- pens as a result of the heavy increasing. It is weakened if you miss any base chains.

Pom-pom

Cut 2 identical circles of card-board with a hole in the middle. Wind the yarn firmly round both circles, holding them until the centre hole is well filled. Insert scissors between the 2

pieces of cardboard and cut the threads all round. Tie the threads very tightly between the pieces of cardboard, then remove these. Fluff up and trim the pom-pom.

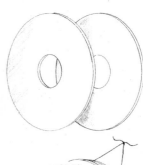
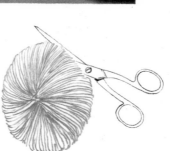

Washing

See the ball band for instructions regarding washing or dry cleaning. When in doubt, wash by hand; use well dissolved soap or detergent designed for knitwear and hand-hot water. Massage and squeeze the fabric gently, never rubbing, scrubbing or twisting. Rinse it extremely well in many changes of water and press out the water against the side of the bowl afterwards. (Never try to lift or handle saturated fabric.) A quick spell in a spin-drier is a good way to shorten the drying time. Lay the article on a towel spread on a flat surface, pat it into shape and leave it to dry away from direct heat or sunlight. Nearly dry crochet fabric may survive being draped over a line or a drying rack, but never peg it by the shoulders or extremities.

AMANDA'S MUSHROOMS
BEACH BOLERO
SOLOMON'S KNOT CURTAIN

These three varied projects are simple enough for a beginner and yet offer plenty of scope for creative experimenting.

Amanda's Mushrooms

12 year old Amanda has created a whole collection of fantastic crochet fungi, which make lovely presents for friends and relations. She was inspired originally by colourful illustrations in books and often returns from a walk in the countryside with an interesting specimen. As they only use small quantities of yarn, she uses up oddments from her mother's workbasket. When asked how she made them, she replied 'They are very easy. You just need a rounded top, a bit of stalk, and a sort of base, like an upturned saucer, only an oval . . . and there you are.'

BRITISH PATTERN
'Rounded top'
Make 3 ch, sl st to form a ring.
1st round. 3 ch, 10 tr into ring, sl st to top of 3 ch.
2nd round. 3 ch, 1 tr in each tr, sl st to top of 3 ch.
3rd round. 2 ch, tr 2 tog all round, sl st to top of 2 ch.
To make a larger version, work 2 tr in each st on 2nd round. Change colour and work 2 rounds as 3rd round.

'Stalk'
Do not fasten off, but insert hook through rem hole in under layer of Top, pick up thread of the underside of top layer and work sl st to draw layers tog. Work ch length required for stalk, turn and work back in dc over ch. (For larger version use htr.) Sl st to underside of Top, then sl st firmly back down stalk, going through both loops of dc tog with base ch. Fasten off, leaving yarn to sew to base. Push Top into shape.

'Base'
Using yarn to represent grass, work as for larger version of Top for 2 rounds.
3rd round. 1 dc in each of next 5 sts, 1 tr in next 5 sts, 1 dc in next 5 sts, 1 tr in rem sts. Fasten off.
Make a group of different mushrooms and sew into a base. Stiffen stalks with short pieces of plastic covered wire. Different thicknesses of yarns will produce a variety of sizes: the chunkier yarns make a more stable mushroom, while fine cottons will produce a really delicate one, and their charm lies in the fact that no two will be alike.

AMERICAN PATTERN
'Rounded top'
Make 3 ch, sl st to form a ring.
1st round. 3 ch, 10 dc into ring, sl st to top of 3 ch.
2nd round. 3 ch, 1 dc in each dc, sl st to top of 3 ch.
3rd round. 2 ch, dc 2 tog all around, sl st to top of 2 ch.
To make a larger version, work 2 dc in each st on 2nd round. Change color and work 2 rounds as 3rd round.

'Stalk'
Do not fasten off, but insert hook through remaining hole in under layer of Top, pick up thread of the underside of top layer and work sl st to draw layers tog. Work ch length required for stalk, turn and work back in sc over ch. (For larger version use hdc.) Sl st to underside of Top, then sl st firmly back down stalk, going through both loops of sc tog with base ch. Fasten off, leaving yarn to sew to base. Push Top into shape.

'Base'
Using yarn to represent grass, work as for larger version of Top for 2 rounds.
3rd round. 1 sc in each of next 5 sts, 1 dc in next 5 sts, 1 sc in next 5 sts, 1 dc in remaining sts. Fasten off.
To make a group of mushrooms, see British pattern.

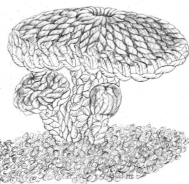

Beach Bolero

This sleeveless top has been designed to suit a beginner. It incorporates 4 of the basic stitches, chain, slip stitch, double crochet [single crochet] and half treble [half double crochet] so you can be practising these and making something to wear at the same time. There is no need to worry about tension [gauge] and there is no shaping as the 2 halves of the garment are simply straight strips which are joined at the back and sides. The base chain of each strip is worked to an approximate width and then edgings are worked afterwards until the strip fits your requirements. This project gives complete freedom in choice of stitch and yarn. The top illustrated was made in a medium weight crochet cotton similar in thickness to a double knitting [knitting worsted] yarn, and using a 4.00 mm [F] hook.

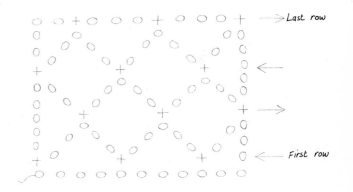

BRITISH PATTERN
[American Pattern in brackets]
The strips (make 2)
Work base chain loosely to measure approx 26 cm (10 in). Use larger hook if necessary to obtain a loose base chain.
Base row. Work 1 dc [1 sc] into 8th ch from hook * 5 ch, miss [skip] 3 ch of the base ch, 1 dc [1 sc] in next ch, rep from * until work measures approx 18 cm (7 in) wide. If any spare sts remain of base ch, ignore them. Turn work.
Patt row. 7 ch, 1 dc [1 sc] in 1st loop (i.e. work into hole formed by ch) * 5 ch, 1 dc [1 sc] in next loop, rep from * to end. Turn. Rep patt row to length required for Front and Back combined – approx 115 cm (45 in) for an average adult. If you are working a suitable stitch pattern and would like simple pockets, work an extra 10 or 12 cm (4 or 5 in). Then work last row: 4 ch, 1 dc [1 sc] in 1st loop, * 3 ch, 1 dc [1 sc] in next loop, rep from * to end. Fasten off.

Edgings
To obtain correct measurement, add 5 cm (2 in) to your bust/chest measurement and divide by 4 to find the necessary width of each strip; e.g. to fit 87 cm (34 in), strip will need to be 23 cm (9 in). The strips will already be approx 15–20 cm (6–8 in) so make up the difference by adding half the extra required to each edge, that is working an equal number of rows along each side. If extra length has been worked for pocket, fold up the extra portion and pin in place.
1st row. (right side facing) Join yarn at corner, 2 ch, work in htr [hdc] evenly along edge of strip, inserting hook through both thicknesses along pocket edge, if any. The number of stitches depends on tension [gauge] and yarn used, so experiment and lay work flat from time to time to ensure the edge remains straight. Turn.
2nd row. 2 ch, 1 htr [1 hdc] in each st to end. Turn. Rep 2nd row to required measurement. Complete edging on other side of strip in the same way, and rep on 2nd strip.

To make up [finish]
Fold each strip in half. Join strip tog along 1 side from end towards fold, either by sewing or sl st, inserting hook through both thicknesses and working sts loosely, leaving 23 cm (9 in) open for armhole. Join the 2 strips tog in the same way at centre back, ending 10 cm (4 in) from fold.

With right side facing, join yarn to lower left front, and work 1 row in htr [hdc] round lower edge of garment.
Note. If there are any spare ch from base ch, unpick [unravel], and encase loose ends in this row.
Patch pockets, belt or fastenings can be added to this basic garment.

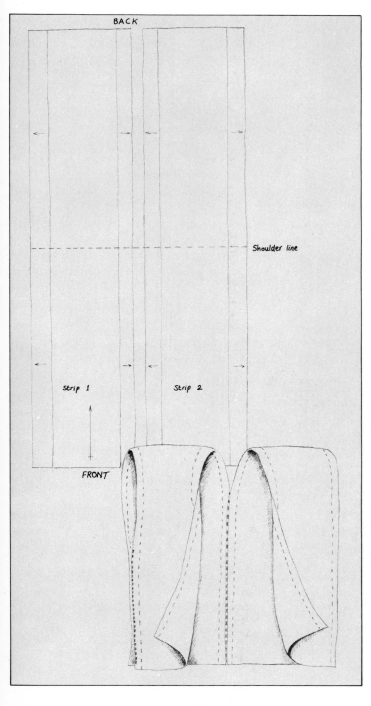

Solomon's Knot Curtain

The success of this project depends on using a wide variety of different yarns, both thick and thin, plain and textured, matt and shiny, etc. The curtain illustrated on page 39 contains 15 types.

MATERIALS
Yarn: You will require roughly 230 gm per square metre (6¾ oz per square yard), but to begin with, buy 1 ball each of at least 10 different qualities, start making the curtain, then buy more later if necessary. (Slight variations in dyelot do not matter in this project.)

Curtain rings: 1 ring per 7.5 cm (3 in) of span of curtain plus 1. Allow more for greater density of fabric.

Dowel rod to fit rings comfortably; length as span of curtains. This is used to support the curtain while you are working.

Crochet hooks in various sizes to suit yarns.
Note. The curtain is made from the top downwards. Select one or more strands of yarn for each row as desired. Use an appropriate hook for each yarn. With an uneven yarn, use a hook to suit thickest part.

BRITISH PATTERN
Base row. With a medium thickness yarn and hook, make a slip knot on hook, * work (1 tr, 1 ch, 1 tr – called V st) into curtain ring, 1 ch, pull loop on hook through to approx 18 cm (7 in), yrh, pull through to complete a loose ch, insert hook in back thread of ch and make dc – Solomon's knot made.
Rep from * ending 1 V st into last curtain ring. Fasten off.
Thread rings on to dowel rod and suspend dowel from either end by adjustable strings to facilitate working.
Patt row. Using various yarns as desired, work V sts as for base row, but working into the centre of previous V st and varying the size of V st to suit yarn as foll: for medium or thin yarns work (1 dtr, 1 ch, 1 dtr) and for thick yarns work (1 tr, 1 ch, 1 tr). Since the fabric is hanging upside down, pick up each V st as you come to it with your left hand and turn it right way up towards you. Then insert the hook under the centre chain and between the 2 vertical stitches. If you require some rows to curve or zigzag, use longer then shorter sts in the V sts.

Support threads. In order to support fabric or adjust length, work in surface slip st, with your least stretchy yarn. Comm from a curtain ring and work down centre of a line of V sts to lower edge. Use long sts, approx 1 st per row, and tighten as desired. The curtain illustrated has support threads from every 4th ring.
Edges. Work 1 or more rows in dc, encasing loose ends.

AMERICAN PATTERN
Base row. With a medium thickness yarn and hook, make a slip knot on hook, * work (1 dc, 1 ch, 1 dc – called V st) into curtain ring, 1 ch, pull loop on hook through to approx 18 cm (7 in), yo, draw through to complete a loose ch, insert hook in back thread of ch and make 1 sc – Solomon's knot made.
Rep from * ending 1 V st into last curtain ring. Fasten off. Thread rings on to dowel rod and suspend dowel from either end by adjustable strings to facilitate working.
Pat row. Using various yarns as desired, work V sts as for base row, but working into the center of previous V st and varying the size of V st to suit yarn as follows: for medium or thin yarns work (1 tr, 1 ch, 1 tr) and for thick yarns work (1 dc, 1 ch, 1 dc). Since the fabric is hanging upside down, pick up each V st as you come to it with your left hand and turn it right way up towards you. Then insert the hook under the center chain and between the 2 vertical stitches.
If you require some rows to curve or zigzag, use longer then shorter sts in the V sts.
Support threads. See British pat.
Edges. Work 1 or more rows in sc, encasing loose ends.

CROCHET BORDERS
LACY COLLAR
BEACH BAG

Deep crocheted borders give simple hand towels a luxurious look and are especially effective all in white. The three different patterns are each given in two versions: a deep one for hand towels and a narrow one for guest towels. Crocheted in thick cotton, they can be worked quickly, and diagrams make the patterns easy to follow.

Little girls like lace trimmings too. This lacy collar can simply be tied at the neck of a party dress and looks equally pretty over a colourful floral print or smart navy blue velvet. The flowers and circles are crocheted individually and then sewn together; a crocheted border gives the collar its shape.

Crochet in a bolder mood is illustrated by this brightly coloured beach bag, made from strips of cotton fabric which you may already have left over from dressmaking.

Crochet Borders

Deep Border: Length 50 cm (19½ in) Depth 9–10 cm (3½–4 in)
Narrow Border: Length 30 cm (12 in) Depth 5 cm (2 in)

MATERIALS
Yarn: 100 gm (4 oz) medium
crochet cotton for deep
border
50 gm (2 oz) for narrow
border

2.50 mm [B] crochet hook

KEY to DIAGRAMS

o	=	1 chain
+	=	1 dc [sc]
†	=	1 tr [dc]
‡	=	1 dtr [tr]
	=	1 cr tr [cr dc]
⌒	=	1 sl st
	=	1 picot (4 ch, 1 dc [1 sc] into 1st ch)

BRITISH PATTERN [American
pattern in brackets]

SCALLOPS
Narrow Border (worked sideways)
Make 6 ch, plus 3 ch for turning.
Follow diagram, work to end of 3rd row.
To work curve. 5 ch, sl st in top of turning ch on 2nd row, 1 ch, sl st to tr [dc] on 1st row, turn, * 1 ch, 1 tr [dc], rep 5 times in all in loop. Cont with 4th row.
Rep 2nd to 5th rows 7 times, and end with 6th to 9th rows.
Work 1 row picot on curved edge, and finish other edges with 1 row dc [sc].

SCALLOPS
Deep Border (worked sideways)
Make 10 ch, plus 3 ch for turning.
Follow diagram, work to end of 5th row.
To work curve. 5 ch, sl st in top of turning ch on 4th row, 1 ch, sl st in tr [dc] on 3rd row, turn, 10 tr [dc] in loop, cont with 6th row on diagram. Work 7th and 8th rows to correspond.
Rep 2nd to 9th rows 6 times, and end with 10th to 17th rows.
Work 1 row picot on curved edge, and finish other edges with 1 row dc [sc].

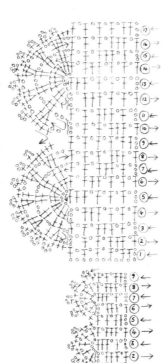

WAVES
Deep Border
Make 129 ch, plus 1 ch for turning.
Follow diagram.
To finish, work dc [sc] along both ends of border.

Narrow Border
Make 69 ch, plus 1 ch for turning.
Follow diagram, work 3rd row. Work 8th to 11th rows.
To finish, work dc [sc] along both ends of border.

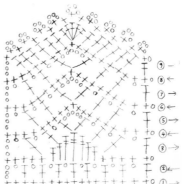

SHELLS
Deep Border
Make 118 ch, plus 1 ch for turning.
Follow diagram.
To finish, work dc [sc] along both ends of border.

Narrow Border
Make 73 ch, plus 1 ch for turning.
Follow diagram, work 5th to 9th rows.
To finish, work dc [sc] along both ends of border.

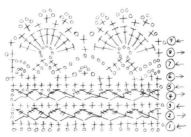

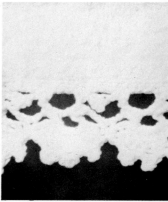

Lacy Collar

Neck size: 32 cm (13 in)

MATERIALS

Yarn: 50 gm (2 oz) No. 10 (fine) crochet cotton

1.50 mm [steel 7] crochet hook

BRITISH PATTERN

Flower

Make 8 ch, sl st to form a ring.

1st round. 3 ch, for 1st tr, 15 tr into ring, sl st to top of 3 ch.

2nd round. 1 ch, * 1 dc in next tr, 5 ch, miss 1 tr, rep from * 7 times more, sl st to 1st dc.

3rd round. 1 ch, * 1 dc, 5 tr, 1 dc into 5 ch loop, rep from * 7 times more, sl st to 1st dc.
Fasten off.

Circle

Make 10 ch, sl st to form a ring.

1st round. 2 ch for 1st htr, 18 htr into ring, sl st to top of 2 ch. Fasten off.

Make 11 flowers and sew tog in a row, with 1 petal touching. Make 10 circles and sew between flowers joining each circle to 2 petals.

Upper edge

1st row. Make 6 ch, 1 tr in top petal of 1st flower, * 11 ch, 1 tr in top petal of next flower, * rep from * to * twice, 9 ch, 1 tr in top petal of next flower, rep from * to * twice, 9 ch, 1 tr in top petal of next flower, rep from * to * 3 times, 6 ch. Turn.

2nd row. 1 ch, 1 dc in each ch and tr to end of row. Turn.

3rd row. 3 ch for 1st tr, * 1 ch, miss 1 dc, 1 tr in next dc, rep from * to end. Turn.

4th row. 1 ch, 1 dc in each ch and tr to end of row. Fasten off.

Lower edge

Join yarn to corner of upper edge.

1st row. 7 ch, 1 tr in 1st free petal of 1st flower, 11 ch, 1 tr in next petal, 9 ch, 1 tr in 3rd petal, 7 ch, 1 tr in 4th petal, * 11 ch, 1 dc in circle, 11 ch, 1 tr in next petal, rep from * twice, 11 ch, 1 dc in circle, ** 9 ch, 1 tr in next petal, 9 ch, 1 dc in circle, rep from ** twice, 11 ch, 1 dc in next petal, rep from * 3 times, 7 ch, 1 tr in next petal, 9 ch, 1 tr in next petal 11 ch, 1 tr in next petal, 7 ch, 1 dc, 1 ch, 1 dc in side of upper edge.

2nd and 3rd rows. As 2nd and 3rd rows of Upper Edge.

4th row. 1 ch, 1 dc in tr, 1 dc in ch, * 4 ch, 1 dc in 1st ch (picot), miss 1 tr, 1 dc in each next ch, tr, and ch, rep from * to end of row. Fasten off.

Ties

Make 80 ch, work 1 row dc. Fasten off. Sew ties to collar.

AMERICAN PATTERN

Flower

Make 8 ch, sl st to form a ring.

1st round. 3 ch, for 1st dc, 15 dc into ring, sl st to top of 3 ch.

2nd round. 1 ch, * 1 sc in next dc, 5 ch, skip 1 dc, rep from * 7 times more, sl st to 1st sc.

3rd round. 1 ch, * 1 sc, 5 dc, 1 sc into 5 ch loop, rep from * 7 times more, sl st to 1st sc. Fasten off.

Circle

Make 10 ch, sl st to form a ring.

1st round. 2 ch for 1st hdc, 18 hdc into ring, sl st to top of 2 ch. Fasten off. Make 11 flowers and sew tog in a row, with 1 petal touching. Make 10 circles and sew between flowers joining each circle to 2 petals.

Upper edge

1st row. Make 6 ch, 1 dc in top petal of 1st flower, * 11 ch, 1 dc in top petal of next flower, * rep from * to * twice, 9 ch, 1 dc in top petal of next flower, rep from * to * twice, 9 ch, 1 dc in top petal of next flower, rep from * to * 3 times, 6 ch. Turn.

2nd row. 1 ch, 1 sc in ch and dc to end of row. Turn.

3rd row. 3 ch for 1st dc, * 1 ch, skip 1 sc, 1 dc in next sc, rep from * to end. Turn.

4th row. 1 ch, 1 sc in each ch and dc to end of row. Fasten off.

Lower edge

Join yarn to corner of upper edge.

1st row. 7 ch, 1 dc in 1st free petal of 1st flower, 11 ch, 1 dc in next petal, 9 ch, 1 dc in 3rd petal, 7 ch, 1 dc in 4th petal, * 11 ch, 1 sc in circle, 11 ch, 1 dc in next petal, rep from * twice, 11 ch, 1 sc in circle, ** 9 ch, 1 dc in next petal, 9 ch, 1 sc in circle, rep from ** twice, 11 ch, 1 sc in next petal, rep from * 3 times, 7 ch, 1 dc in next petal, 9 ch, 1 dc in next petal, 11 ch, 1 dc in next petal, 7 ch, 1 sc, 1 ch, 1 sc in side of upper edge.

2nd and 3rd rows. As 2nd and 3rd rows of Upper Edge.

4th row. 1 ch, 1 sc in dc, 1 sc in ch, * 4 ch, 1 sc in 1st ch (picot), skip 1 dc, 1 sc in each next ch, dc, and ch, rep from * to end of row. Fasten off.

Ties

Make 80 ch, work 1 row sc. Fasten off. Sew ties to collar.

Beach Bag

TENSION [GAUGE]

6 sts and 6 rows to 10 cm (4 in) worked on a 9 mm [13 wood] hook.

MATERIALS

Remnants of thin cotton materials in assorted patterns and colours.

9 mm [13 wood] crochet hook.

BRITISH PATTERN

Cut or tear material into strips 4 cm (1½ in) wide, and sew pieces firmly tog into continuous strip, arranging colours and patterns to taste.
Make 3 ch.

1st round. (1 dc in 1 ch) twice, 2 dc in 3rd ch, cont along other side of ch (1 dc in 1 ch) twice, 2 dc in last ch, sl st to 1st dc. (8 sts)

2nd round. * (1 dc in next st) twice, (2 dc in next st) twice, * rep from * to * once, sl st to 1st dc. (12 sts)

3rd round. * (1 dc in next st) twice, (2 dc in next st) 4 times, * rep from * to * once, sl st to 1st dc. (20 sts)

4th & 5th rounds. Inc 6 sts in each round, working inc over inc of previous round. (32 sts)

6th, 7th, 8th & 9th rounds. Inc 4 sts on each round. (48 sts)

10th, 11th & 12th rounds. Inc 2 sts on each round. (54 sts)
Work 10 rounds without further shaping.
Fasten off and sew end of fabric strip securely to bag. Make 2 plaits of fabric 40 cm (16 in) long, or required length, and sew firmly to bag for handles.

AMERICAN PATTERN

Cut or tear material into strips 1½ in wide, and sew pieces firmly tog into continuous strip, arranging colors and patterns to taste.
Make 3 ch.

1st round. (1 sc in 1 ch) twice, 2 sc in 3rd ch, continue along other side of ch, (1 sc in 1 ch) twice, 2 sc in last ch, sl st to 1st sc. (8 sts)

2nd round. * (1 sc in next st) twice, (2 sc in next st) twice * rep from * to * once, sl st in 1st sc. (12 sts)

3rd round. * (1 sc in next st) twice, (2 sc in next st) 4 times * rep from * to * once, sl st to 1st sc. (20 sts)

4th & 5th rounds. Inc 6 sts in each round, working inc over inc of previous round. (32 sts)

6th, 7th, 8th and 9th rounds. Inc 4 sts on each round. (48 sts)

10th, 11th & 12th rounds. Inc 2 sts on each round. (54 sts)
Work 10 rounds without further shaping. Fasten off and sew end of fabric strip securely to bag.
Make 2 braids of fabric 16 in long, or the required length, and sew them firmly to bag for handles.

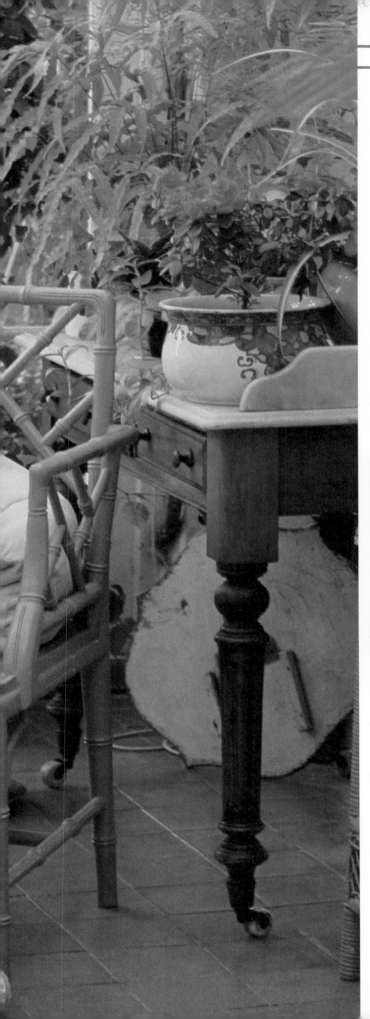

DECORATIVE TRIMMINGS
CROCHET SOCKS

Versatile crochet motifs can be used in all sorts of interesting ways. Here they've been joined to make trimmings for a woman's apron and a child's dress – both made in cool cotton for summertime comfort. Complete instructions for making and inserting the trimmings are given on the following pages.
Also ideal for summer are these filet crochet socks – just the thing to wear with sandals.

Decorative Trimmings for Child's Dress

Chest: 69/71 cm (27/28 in)

BRITISH PATTERN

Make 14 motifs (see instructions opposite) and join by sewing 2 petals of each flower together.

Upper edge

1st row. 8 ch, * sl st in centre tr of 1st petal, 5 ch, sl st in centre tr of 2nd petal, 8 ch, rep from * to end of row, ending with 10 ch. Turn.
2nd row. 1 tr in 3rd ch from hook, 1 tr in every ch to end of row, 2 ch. Turn.
3rd row. 1 tr in every tr, 5 ch. Turn.
4th row. Miss 3 tr, 1 tr in next tr, * 3 ch, miss 3 tr, 1 tr in next tr, rep from * to end, 2 ch. Turn.
5th row. * 1 tr in each of 3 ch, 1 tr in tr, rep from * to end of row. Fasten off.

Lower edge

Work 1st to 3rd rows inclusive of upper edging.
Fasten off.
Rejoin yarn to base of tr at end of lower edging.
1st row. 8 ch, sl st in centre tr of 1st petal, 5 ch, sl st in centre of 2nd petal, 8 ch, 6 sl st in side of upper edging. Turn.
2nd row. Sl st across 6 sts, 14 ch, 4 sl st, across lower edging, 2 ch. Turn.
Working 1 tr in each st, work 4 rows of tr in all. Fasten off.
Complete other end to match.
Make 2 buttonholes with ch along one end, and work over ch loops in dc to strengthen.

Pocket

Make 3 motifs and join tog as before. Edge motifs as before, starting with 5 ch. Work 2 rows in tr on upper edge and 1 row in tr on lower edge.

Shoulder straps (make 4)

Join yarn to upper edging.
Make ch the required length.
1st row. 1 tr in every ch.
2nd row. 1 dc in every tr along both sides of strap. Fasten off.

AMERICAN PATTERN

Make 14 motifs (see opposite) and join by sewing 2 petals of each flower together.

Upper edge

1st row. 8 ch, * sl st in center dc of 1st petal, 5 ch, sl st in center dc of 2nd petal, 8 ch, rep from * to end of row, ending with 10 ch. Turn.
2nd row. 1 dc in 3rd ch from hook, 1 dc in every ch to end of row, 2 ch. Turn.
3rd row. 1 dc in every dc, 5 ch. Turn.
4th row. Skip 3 dc, 1 dc in next dc, * 3 ch.
Skip 3 dc, 1 dc in next dc, rep from * to end, 2 ch. Turn.
5th row. * 1 dc in each of 3 ch, 1 dc in dc, rep from * to end of row. Fasten off.

Lower edge

Work 1st to 3rd rows inclusive of upper edging. Fasten off.
Rejoin yarn at base of dc at end of lower edging.
1st row. 8 ch, sl st in center dc of 1st petal, 5 ch, sl st in center of dc of 2nd petal, 8 ch, 6 sl st in side of upper edging. Turn.
2nd row. Sl st across 6 sts, 14 ch, 4 sl st across lower edging, 2 ch. Turn.
Working 1 dc in each st, work 4 rows in dc in all.
Fasten off.
Complete other end to match.
Make 2 buttonholes with ch along one end, and work over ch loops in sc to strengthen.

Pocket

Make 3 motifs and join tog as before. Edge motifs as before, starting with 5 ch.
Work 2 rows in dc on upper edge, and 1 row in dc on lower edge.

Shoulder straps (make 4)

Join yarn to upper edging.
Make ch the required length.
1st row. 1 dc in every ch.
2nd row. 1 sc in every dc along both sides of strap.
Fasten off.

Woman's apron

1. Turn under 6 mm (¼ in) and then a further 1 cm (⅜ in) on bib side and top edges, skirt side edges and pocket top edge and machine stitch.
2. Neaten bib and skirt waist raw edges by turning under 6 mm (¼ in) and machine stitch close to edge. Turn over a further 1 cm (⅜ in) and baste.
3. Turn under 1 cm (⅜ in) on pocket raw edges and baste. Stitch pockets in place.
4. At skirt hem edge turn under 1 cm (⅜ in) and then a further 4 cm (1½ in) and stitch.
5. Pin 1 cm (⅜ in) deep tucks on bib and skirt back and front. On the skirt, 5 cm (2 in) in from edge and then two at
4 cm (1½ in) intervals. On bib at 2 cm (¾ in) in from edge and two more at 1.3 cm (½ in) intervals. On the wrong side, oversew the tucks by hand.
6. Stitch side tab sections together, leaving opening for turning through. Turn to right side and slip stitch opening.
7. Baste crochet insertion to right side of skirt top and bib, overlapping edges by 1 cm (⅜ in). Baste and stitch side tabs in place and hem crochet.
8. Pin crochet shoulder straps in place; adjust length and hem.

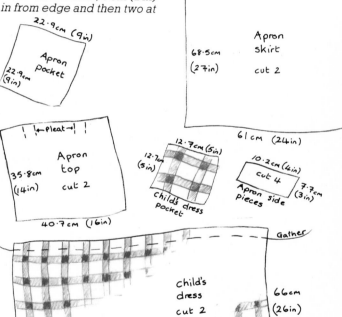

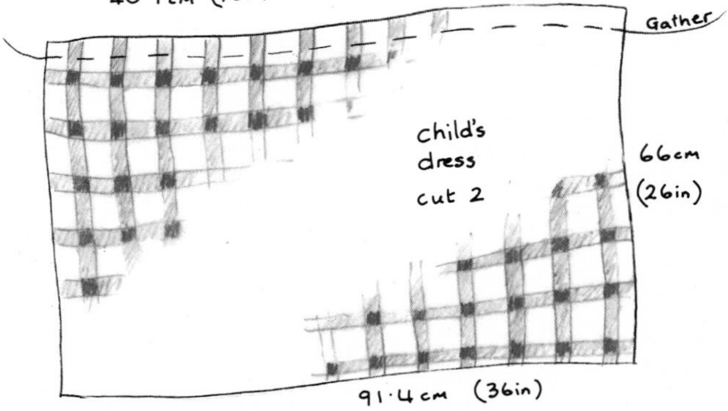

Child's dress

1. On pocket top turn under 1 cm (⅜ in) and then 2 cm (¾ in) and machine stitch. Turn under seam allowance on remaining edges. Press.
2. Sew crochet trimming to pocket by hand. Position on dress and top stitch in place.
3. Join dress pieces with side seams. For back opening, reinforce 10 cm (4 in) slash point with machine stitching. Slash opening. Cut a strip of fabric 4 × 20 cm (1½ × 8 in).
With right sides together, baste and stitch facing strip to opening. Turn over to wrong side, turn under 1 cm (⅜ in) and hem.
4 Work two rows of gathering stitches at top edge of dress. Gather to fit crochet yoke. Neaten raw edge by hand or machine stitching.
5. Position crochet yoke on right side, 1 cm (⅛ in) down from edge, pin and baste. Sew crochet to dress by hand.
6. Sew a press stud at top of back opening. Sew on buttons.

Woman's Apron

BRITISH PATTERN
Waistband (make 2)
Make 8 motifs (see below) and join by sewing 2 petals of each flower together.

Edging
1st row. 5 ch, * sl st in centre tr of 1st petal, 5 ch, sl st in centre tr of 2nd petal, 8 ch, rep from * to end. Turn.
2nd row. 1 tr in 3rd ch from hook, 1 tr in every ch to end of row. 2 ch. Turn.
3rd row. 1 tr in every tr to end. Fasten off.
Rep edging on other long edge.
Rejoin yarn to base of tr at one end, 5 ch, sl st to centre tr of 1st petal, 5 ch, sl st to centre tr of 2nd petal, 5 ch, 4 sl st along side of tr, 2 ch. Turn. Work 4 tr in side of tr and 1 tr in each ch, work 2 rows of tr in all. Fasten off.
Complete other end to match.

Shoulder straps (make 2)
Make 5 motifs and sew tog as before.
Work edging as for waistband, but working only 1 row of tr on edges and 3 rows of tr at ends.

AMERICAN PATTERN
Waistband (make 2)
Make 8 motifs (see below) and join by sewing 2 petals of each flower together.

Edging
1st row. 5 ch, * sl st in center dc of 1st petal, 5 ch, sl st in center dc of 2nd petal, 8 ch, rep from * to end. Turn.
2nd row. 1 dc in 3rd ch from hook, 1 dc in every ch to end of row. 2 ch. Turn.
3rd row. 1 dc in every dc to end. Fasten off. Repeat edging on other long edge.
Rejoin yarn to base of dc at one end, 5 ch, sl st to center dc of 1st petal, 5 ch, sl st to center dc of 2nd petal, 5 ch, 4 sl, st along side of dc, 2 ch. Turn. Work 4 dc in side of dc and 1 dc in each ch. Work 2 rows of dc in all. Fasten off.
Complete other end to match.

Shoulder straps (make 2)
Make 5 motifs and sew tog as before.
Work edging as for waistband, but working only 1 row of dc on edges, and 3 rows of dc at ends.

Motif for Woman's Apron and Child's Dress

MATERIALS
Yarn: No. 20 (fine) crochet cotton

1.50 mm [steel 7] crochet hook

BRITISH PATTERN
Motif
Make 5 ch, sl st to form a ring.
1st round. 4 ch for 1st dtr, 2 dtr cluster, worked by leaving last loop of each st on hook, yrh, and draw through all loops, * 5 ch, 1 dtr, 2 dtr cl, rep from * 6 times, 5 ch, sl st to top of 4 ch. (8 cls)
2nd round. * 1 dc, 6 tr, 1 dc in 5 ch loop, rep from * 7 times, sl st to 1st dc. Fasten off.

AMERICAN PATTERN
Motif
Make 5 ch, sl st to form a ring.
1st round. 4 ch for 1st tr, 2 tr cluster, worked by leaving last loop of each st on hook, yo, and draw through all loops, * 5 ch, 1 tr, 2 tr cl, rep from * 6 times, 5 ch, sl st to top of 4 ch. (8 cls)
2nd round. * 1 sc, 6 dc, 1 sc in 5 ch loop, rep from * 7 times, sl st to 1st sc. Fasten off.

Crochet Socks

Size: To fit average lady's foot (adjustable)

TENSION [GAUGE]
60 sts and 17 rows to 10 cm (4 in) measured over Filet crochet with No. 1.25 [steel 8] hook.

MATERIALS
Yarn: 30 gm (1½ oz) No. 30 (fine) crochet cotton

1.25mm [8 steel] crochet hook

BRITISH PATTERN
Comm at top of sock, make 108 ch, sl st to form a ring.
Work 25 rounds in Filet crochet, following diagram, starting each round with 2 ch for 1st tr and ending with sl st to top of 2 ch.

Heel
Work 7 rows tr, back and forth over 1st 54 sts. Fasten off. Miss 18 sts, rejoin yarn, work 7 rows tr over centre 18 sts. Fasten off.
Rejoin yarn to top of 7th row of trs at heel, work 1 tr, 2 ch into each row end (21 sts) work 54 sts across leg, 1 tr, 2 ch in each row end of trs (21 sts) 1 tr, 2 ch, across heel (18 sts) 114 sts. Work 1 round.
3rd round. Dec 2 sp on sole thus: * miss 1 tr, work next tr in ch sp, miss 1 tr, work next tr in tr, rep from * once more (108 sts).
Cont until foot is required length.

Toe
Work 5 rounds in tr, taking 2 tr tog at each side of sole on every round. Fasten off. Crochet 1 round picot around upper edge of sock. Join heel and toe seams.

AMERICAN PATTERN
Start at top of sock, make 108 ch, sl st to form a ring.
Work 25 rounds in Filet crochet, following diagram, starting each round with 2 ch for 1st dc and ending with sl st to top of 2 ch.

Heel
Work 7 rows dc, back and forth over 1st 54 sts. Fasten off.
Skip 18 sts, rejoin yarn, work 7 rows dc over center 18 sts. Fasten off.
Rejoin yarn to top of 7th row of dc at heel, work 1 dc, 2 ch into each row end (21 sts), work 54 sts across leg, 1 dc, 2 ch in each row end of dc (21 sts) 1 dc, 2 ch across heel (18 sts) 114 sts. Work 1 round.
3rd round. Dec 2 sp on sole thus: * miss 1 dc, work next dc in ch sp, miss 1 dc, work next dc in dc, rep from * once more (108 sts). Continue until foot is required length.

Toe
Work 5 rounds in dc, taking 2 dc tog at each side of sole on every round. Fasten off. Crochet 1 round picot around upper edge of sock. Join seams.

☐ 1 space (2 ch., miss [skip] 2 sts. tr. [dc.] in next st)
☒ 1 block (3 tr. [3 dc.])

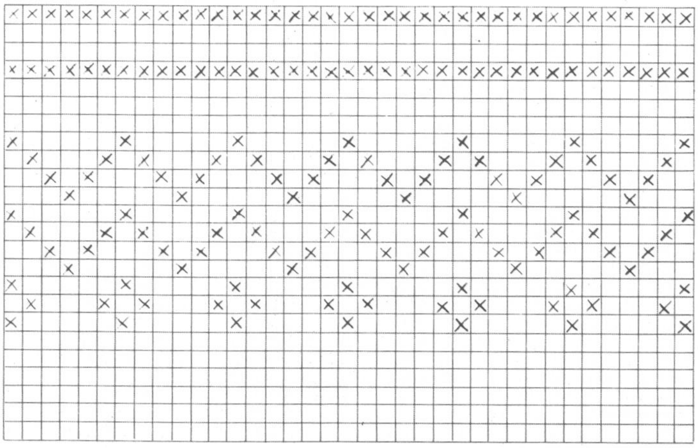

ROSY DOLL
CHILD'S HAT
FILET CURTAIN

Here are two projects designed especially for children. The Rosy doll and woolly hat are easily made, even by beginners, and both can be made up from an assortment of leftover yarns from your workbasket.
For the experienced crocheter, the delicate lace curtain is worked in fine white cotton, using alternating bird and rose motifs.

Rosy Doll

Size: Approx 28 cm (11 in) high

MATERIALS
Yarn: Oddments of double knitting [knitting worsted] yarn

Stuffing

3.50 mm [E] and
3.00 mm [C] crochet hooks

BRITISH PATTERN
Body (make 2)
With 3.00 mm hook and dress colour yarn, make 13 ch.
Work 23 rows in dc. Fasten off. Change to flesh colour, join yarn to 5th dc.
1st row. 5 dc. Turn.
2nd row. 5 dc, 5 ch. Turn.
3rd row. 1 dc in each ch, 5 dc, 5 ch. Turn.
4th row. 1 dc in each ch, dc to end. (15 sts)
Work 7 rows in dc.
Cont in dc, dec 1 st at beg of every row until 4 sts rem. Work 1 row in dc. Fasten off.

Arms (make 2)
With 3.00 mm hook and flesh colour yarn, make 11 ch.
Work 6 rows in dc.
Change to dress colour, work 15 rows in dc. Fasten off.

Legs (make 2)
With 3.00 mm hook and dress colour, make 15 ch.
Work 6 rows in dc.
Change to flesh colour, work 15 rows in dc. Fasten off.

Collar
With 3.50 mm hook and dress colour, make 15 ch. Work 1 row in tr. (13 sts) Fasten off.

Skirt
With 3.50 mm hook and dress colour, make 40 ch.
Work 12 rows in tr. Fasten off.

Hat
With 3.50 mm hook and white yarn, make 4 ch, sl st to form ring.
Work 10 dc into ring, sl st to 1st dc. Work 7 rounds in dc, working twice into every alt st. Work 2 rounds in tr. Fasten off.

To make up
Join body sections together, leaving openings on each side for arms. Stuff body through openings. Join arms, stuff, and sew to body. Draw up at wrist. Join legs, stuff, sew to lower body with seam at back of leg. Gather hat between 2 rounds of tr, and sew to head. Join skirt, gather at top and sew to waist. Sew collar in place. Embroider features on face. Knot strands of yarn to head for hair.

AMERICAN PATTERN
Body (make 2)
With size C hook and flesh color yarn, make 13 ch.
Work 23 rows in sc. Fasten off. Change to flesh color, join yarn to 5th sc.
1st row. 5 sc. Turn.
2nd row. 5 sc, 5 ch. Turn.
3rd row. 1 sc in each ch, 5 sc, 5 ch. Turn.
4th row. 1 sc in each ch, sc to end. (15 sts)
Work 7 rows in sc.
Continue in sc, dec 1 st at beg of every row until 4 sts rem. Work 1 row in sc. Fasten off.

Arms (make 2)
With size C hook and flesh color, make 11 ch.
Work 6 rows in sc.
Change to dress color, work 15 rows in sc. Fasten off.

Legs (make 2)
With size C hook and dress color, make 15 ch.
Work 6 rows in sc.
Change to flesh color, work 15 rows in sc. Fasten off.

Collar
With size E hook and dress color, make 15 ch.
Work 1 row in dc. (13 sts) Fasten off.

Skirt
With size E hook and dress color, make 40 ch.
Work 12 rows in dc. Fasten off.

Hat
With size E hook and white yarn, make 4 ch, sl st to form a ring.
Work 10 sc into ring, sl st to 1st sc. Work 7 rounds in sc, working twice into every other st. Work 2 rounds in dc. Fasten off.

To finish
Join body sections together, leaving openings on each side for arms. Stuff body through openings. Join arms, stuff, and sew to body. Draw up at wrist. Join legs, stuff, sew to lower body with seam at back of leg. Gather hat between 2 rounds of dc, and sew to head. Join skirt, gather at top and sew to waist. Sew collar in place. Embroider features on face. Knot strands of yarn to head for hair.

Child's Hat

Size: 46 cm (18 in) around head

MATERIALS
Yarn: 40 gm (1½ oz) double knitting [knitting worsted] in Yellow
40 gm (1½ oz) in Navy

4.00 mm [F] crochet hook

BRITISH PATTERN
With Yellow, make 3 ch, sl st to form a ring.
1st round. 1 ch, 11 htr in ring, sl st to 1 ch.
2nd and 3rd rounds. 1 ch, * 1 htr in next st, 2 htr in next st, rep from * to end, sl st to 1 ch.
4th and 5th rounds. 1 ch, * (1 htr in next st) twice, 2 htr in next st, rep from * to end, sl st to 1 ch.
6th round. 1 ch, * (1 htr in next st) 3 times, 2 htr in next st, rep from * to end, sl st to 1 ch.
7th round. 1 ch, * (1 htr in next st) 4 times, 2 htr in next st, rep from * to end, sl st to 1 ch.
8th and 9th rounds. Work in htr, inc 2 sts evenly in each round.
Work 8 more rounds in htr. Change to Navy, work 16 rounds in htr. Fasten off. Roll up brim.

AMERICAN PATTERN
With Yellow, make 3 ch, sl st to form a ring.
1st round. 1 ch, 11 hdc in ring, sl st to 1 ch.
2nd and 3rd rounds. 1 ch, * 1 hdc in next st, 2 hdc in next st, rep from * to end, sl st to 1 ch.
4th and 5th rounds. 1 ch, * (1 hdc in next st) twice, 2 hdc in next st, rep from * to end, sl st to 1 ch.
6th round. 1 ch, * (1 hdc in next st) 3 times, 2 hdc in next st, rep from * to end, sl st to 1 ch.
7th round. 1 ch, * (1 hdc in next st) 4 times, 2 hdc in next st, rep from * to end, sl st to 1 ch.
8th and 9th rounds. Work in hdc, inc 2 sts evenly in each round.
Work 8 more rounds in hdc. Change to Navy, work 16 rounds in hdc. Fasten off. Roll up brim.

Filet Curtain

Length: 185 cm (73 in)
Width: 97 cm (38 in)

TENSION [GAUGE]
51 sts and 19 rows to 10 cm (4 in) worked in filet crochet on a 1.25 mm [8 steel] hook.
Motif measures 22 cm by 28 cm (8½ in by 11 in).

MATERIALS
Yarn: 480 gm (17 oz) No. 70 (fine) crochet cotton

10 curtain rings 1.5 cm (½ in) diameter

1.25 mm [8 steel] crochet hook

BRITISH PATTERN
Motif
Make 115 ch.
1st row. 1 tr into 7th ch from hook, * 2 ch, miss 2 ch, 1 tr in next ch, rep from * to end, 2 ch. Turn. (37 sps)
Proceed in Filet crochet (working 2 tr over 2 ch sp) foll chart, and turning with 2 ch for 1st tr.
Make 9 rose and 9 bird motifs.

Border
Make 50 ch.

1st row. 1 tr in 3rd ch from hook, 1 tr in next 2 ch, * 2 ch, miss 2 ch, 1 tr in next ch, rep from * to end, 2 ch. Turn. (1 block, 15 sps)

Foll chart for border. Work 1 row. Inc row. 7 ch, sl st across 3 ch, miss 2 ch, 1 tr in each of next 2 ch, 1 tr in tr, patt to end of row, 2 ch. Turn. On return row, work 1 tr in each of 3 ch at inc. Inc thus and dec by sl st over 3 sts, foll chart and rep patt every 27 rows until border measures approx 4.20 m (4⅔ yds) after a complete patt rep.

To make up
Alternate bird and rose motifs, and arrange 3 motifs across width and 6 motifs deep. Sl st motifs tog on wrong side of work on horizontal joins.

Then join strips tog vertically. Sl st border to centre along both long sides and lower edge, pleating border at lower corners.

Work 1 row dc along top edge. Sew on curtain rings.

AMERICAN PATTERN
Motif
Make 115 ch.

1st row. 1 dc into 7th ch from hook, * 2 ch, skip 2 ch, 1 dc in next ch, rep from * to end, 2 ch. Turn. (37 sps)

Proceed in Filet crochet (working 2 dc over 2 ch sp) following chart, and turning with 2 ch for 1st dc.

Make 9 rose and 9 bird motifs.

Border
Make 50 ch.

1st row. 1 dc in 3rd ch from hook, 1 dc in next 2 ch, * 2 ch, skip 2 ch, 1 dc in next ch, rep from * to end, 2 ch. Turn. (1 block 15 sps)

Follow chart for border. Work 1 row.

Inc row. 7 ch, sl st across 3 ch, skip 2 ch, 1 dc in each of next 2 ch, 1 dc in dc, pat to end of row, 2 ch. Turn.

On return row, work 1 dc in each of 3 ch at inc.

Inc this way and dec by sl st over 3 sts, follow chart and rep pat every 27 rows until border

measures approximately 4⅔ yards after a complete patt repeat.

To finish
Alternate bird and rose motifs; arrange 3 motifs across width and 6 motifs deep. Sl st motifs tog on wrong side of work on horizontal joinings. Then join strips tog vertically.

Sl st border to center along both long sides and lower edge, pleating border at lower corners.

Work 1 row sc along top edge. Sew on curtain rings.

☐ 1 space (2 ch., miss [skip] 2 sts. tr. [dc.] in next st)

☒ 1 block (3 tr. [3 dc.])

Repeat

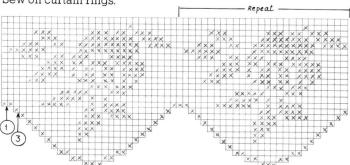

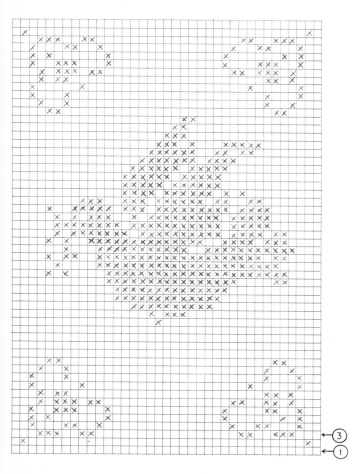

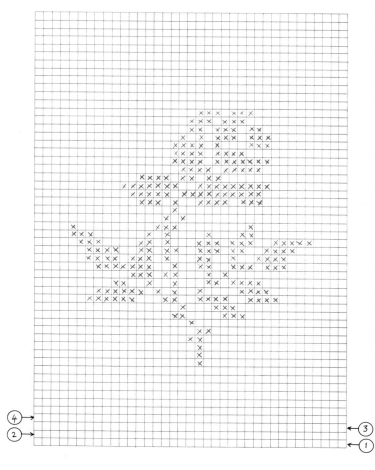

WOODLAND WAISTCOAT

MOHAIR CARDIGAN

TUNISIAN [AFGHAN] JACKET

Three fashionable garments – made in three different ways. The Tunisian [Afghan] jacket (opposite) is worked from a conventional pattern. By contrast, the woodland waistcoat (below left) is worked 'freehand' – the fabric constructed following the shape of a paper pattern and the 'fungi' added in a random fashion according to your own taste. The mohair cardigan is a very simple design worked according to a pattern but using your own selection of yarns to create an original, individual style.

Woodland Waistcoat [Vest]

This waistcoat was inspired by the rich and colourful growths often found on old decaying wood. For this kind of free crochet precise instructions are not possible. Instead, we provide you with guidelines, suggestions and techniques you will need in order to translate the initial inspiration into the final garment. Your waistcoat will therefore differ from ours and will be unique. By using the same approach and techniques you can go on to create your own original designs.

MATERIALS

Yarns. After the first moment of inspiration, one of the most exciting stages in making your own project is searching for the yarns you will need. The types, colours and quantities will depend upon the nature and size of the project. In this case, you will need a wide variety of textured yarns made of wool, mohair and man-made fibres, with brushed, bouclé and chenille construction, as well as standard double knitting [knitting worsted] qualities, in several shades of green, brown, rust, red and black. Because of the quantity of three-dimensional surface crochet work and the rich general texture of the fabric, the finished garment weighs about 550 gm (20 oz).
Four toggles or buttons are required for fastening the waistcoat.
You will need a range of hooks suited to your yarns.

METHOD

As the design is for a waistcoat (it could equally well be a wall hanging), the first task is to draw the whole outline full size on a large piece of paper. (If you are making a wall hanging you may prefer to omit this stage and work quite freely.) Within the outline, roughly sketch in the major features you wish to include, such as the three main groups of fungi. You can, if you like, make detailed sketches and finalize the design at this stage; or you may prefer to work from a general plan only. Often the best work results from 'drawing' directly with the hook and yarn.
Next, decide how to construct the fabric. Study photographs or actual specimens of decaying wood to get an idea of the kinds of textures you want to suggest; for example, the rough surface of tree bark, the velvety surface of moss and the sponge-like qualities of certain fungi. To create the effect of tree bark for the main fabric, simply work conventional rows of straight stitches, but vary the colour and texture by frequently and randomly changing yarns and colours. The section between the shoulders, representing mosses and lichens, calls for a much richer texture in the form of many raised stitches and bobbles as well as frequent changes of yarn. The sharply three-dimensional fungus growths are represented either by surface crochet worked over the background fabric or by separate pieces of crochet which are sewn on later.
The three main sections of the background fabric are made separately. The sections are begun at the lower edge and worked upwards. It is not necessary to do mathematical calculations to obtain the precise size in free crochet – in fact, this approach is usually unreliable. Instead, keep the pattern outline handy on a flat surface and check the work against it frequently as you proceed.
Inserting pockets is easy when, as in this case, you are working in straight horizontal rows. Make a square of the desired size for each pocket lining. When you reach the level of the pocket opening on the garment, work across to the position of the pocket, then work across the upper edge of the pocket lining, bypassing the corresponding number of stitches on the main fabric, and then return to the main fabric to complete the row. When making up the waistcoat, stitch the remaining three edges of the pocket lining in place on the wrong side of the fabric.

The beefsteak fungi (left front). These can also be made beforehand, like the pockets, and attached to the fabric as you go. Hold the piece up to the fabric at the desired position and insert the hook through its edge each time you make a stitch in the fabric, so neatly securing the fungus in place. Or, if you prefer, sew the pieces on after the fabric is complete.
The fungi are simple half circles of fabric made in plain stitches and stripes, but with more increasing than usual to produce the gathered effect.
The bracket fungi (right front). These are worked in surface crochet (see page 30 – 2nd method) with a variety of yarns.
Assorted fungi (back). These can be made both separately and in surface crochet. The caps are half circles – generally 1 row of long stitches, but with fewer stitches than usual, to produce the cupped shape. The stalks may be short lengths of chain, long raised stitches or surface double [single] crochet.

To make up [finish]

Join shoulder seams. Neaten armholes, front, neck and lower edges with 1 row double [single] crochet and 1 row corded edge. At the same time, make ch loops for toggle fastenings. Sew on toggles.

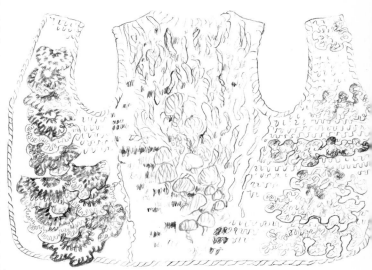

Mohair Cardigan

This garment is the same basic shape as the Beach Bolero – two strips joined together – but the rows run up and down instead of across the width. Choose yarns of various colours and textures, but roughly the same thickness. The top illustrated was made in double knitting weight [knitting worsted]. An interesting effect can be achieved by including a few random-dyed yarns and textured ones, such as mohair, bouclé and chenille. Choice of colours is left to individual taste. Although seventeen different yarns are used in our top, ten would produce a similar effect.

TENSION [GAUGE]

It is not necessary to achieve a specific tension, but choose a hook to suit your thickest yarn and work loosely. If you find tension becomes inconsistent with different yarns, change hooks accordingly. If, however, you prefer to calculate tension before commencing make a tension square with at least 35 stitches.

MATERIALS

Yarn: Approx 500 gm (18 oz) assorted double knitting weight [knitting worsted] yarns

3 buttons 1.5 cm (⅝ in) diameter

5.00 mm [H] crochet hook

BRITISH PATTERN

[American pattern in brackets]
Choose whatever solid stitch pattern you like. With textured yarns it is advisable to use simple stitches. We used combinations of dc, htr, tr, and dtr [sc, hdc, dc, and tr] worked at random to bring out the textures. For added texture we have included some bobbles. Try and avoid working more than one row at a time with the same yarn.

The strips (make 2)

Commence at sides and work both strips towards centre of garment. Make a double chain the required length of garment (front and back combined – approx 117 cm (46 in) for an average adult). To be sure of making strips the same, work both concurrently adding a row to each in turn.
Continue until each strip measures a quarter of required bust measurement plus 5 cm (2 in). For example, for 91 cm (36 in) bust size, the strips should be 24 cm (9½ in), i.e. 96 cm (38 in) divided by 4. If bobbles are desired, work until strip measures 7.5 cm (3 in) less than final width required. Continue as follows:

1st row. Work in dc [sc].
2nd row. Work in dc [sc] with bobbles every 3rd st.
3rd row. Alternate 1 dc [1 sc] and 1 dtr [1 tr].
4th row. As 2nd row.
End with some more plain rows to accommodate buttons. It is advisable to work the last row on each strip in dc [sc], marking position of buttons on left front edge and working loops (3 ch, miss [skip] 2 sts) to correspond with markers.

Pockets

Choose yarn to match or contrast with main part. Make a double chain approx 13 cm (5 in) long and work in the same way as for strips until pocket is square. Sew pockets to fronts.

To make up [finish]

Fold each strip in half, and join tog at 1 side from lower edge, either by sewing or sl st, inserting hook through both thicknesses and working loosely. Leave 23 cm (9 in) open for armhole. Join strips tog in the same way at centre back, ending 13 cm (5 in) below fold at shoulder line. Sew on buttons to correspond with loops. With right side facing join yarn to lower corner of left front and work 1 row dc [sc] around lower edge. Do not turn, but work 1 row corded edge, dc [sc] worked from right to left.
Armholes: With right side facing, join yarn to underarm seam. Work 1st to 4th rows (inclusive) of Bobble patt. Work row dc [sc].

Tunisian [Afghan] Jacket

Bust: 91/97 cm (36/38 in)
Length: 60 cm (23½ in)
Sleeve Seam: 48 cm (19 in)

TENSION [GAUGE]

14 sts and 6 rows to 10 cm (4 in) worked in patt on 7.00 mm [K] hook

MATERIALS

Yarn: 800 gm (29 oz) lightweight chunky [bulky] yarn such as Twilleys Capricorn [heavyweight mohair]

7.00 mm [K] Tunisian [Afghan] hook

6.00 mm [I] crochet hook

BRITISH PATTERN

[American pattern in brackets]
Note. yrh = yo [US readers]

Back

Comm [starting] at centre back with 7.00 mm hook [K], make 79 ch.
1st row. Miss [skip] 2 ch, * yrh, insert hook in next st, yrh, draw through 2 loops, yrh, draw through 1 loop, leaving this loop on hook, rep from * to end. Do not turn, yrh, draw through 1 loop, * yrh, draw through 2 loops, rep from * to end (78 bars). Do not turn.
2nd row. Miss [skip] 1st st, * insert hook in vertical loop of previous row, yrh, draw through, leave loop on hook, rep from * to end. Do not turn, yrh, draw through 1 loop, * yrh, draw through 2 loops, rep from * to end, 2 ch. Do not turn.
Rep 2 row patt 6 times, then work 1st row once.
Note. Always miss [skip] 1st st, but take care not to miss [skip] last st on outward half of row.
Shape armhole. Sl st over 28 sts, work 2nd row to end, ending at armhole (50 bars).
Rep 2 row patt once more. Fasten off.
Rejoin yarn to centre back, comm [start] with 1st row, rep 2 row patt 6 times in all.
Shape armhole. Work 1st row over 50 sts, leave remaining 28 sts. Work 2nd row once. Fasten off.

Left front

With 7.00 mm [K] hook, make 79 ch. Work as for first half of back.

Right front

With 7.00 mm [K] hook, make 79 ch. Work as for second half of back.

Sleeves

With 7.00 mm [K] hook, make 57 ch. Rep 2 row patt 14 times and then work 1st row once more. Fasten off.

Pockets

With 7.00 mm [K] hook, make 24 ch. Rep 2 row patt 4 times. Change to 6.00 mm [I] hook and work 5 rows in dc [sc]. With right side facing, work 1 row dc [sc] from left to right. Fasten off.

To make up [finish]

Place pockets along side seam, with base of pocket to lower front edge. Sew in position. Join front and back at shoulder for 13 cm (5 in) leaving 16 cm (6 in) for back neck.
Join side and sleeve seams and sew sleeve into armhole.
With 6.00 mm [I] hook, work 5 rows dc [sc] at cuff edge. Work 1 row dc [sc] from left to right. Fasten off.
With 6.00 mm [I] hook and right side facing, comm [start] at side seam, work 5 rows dc [sc] all around jacket edge, inc 3 dc [sc] at corners on fronts. Work 1 row dc [sc] from left to right. Fasten off.

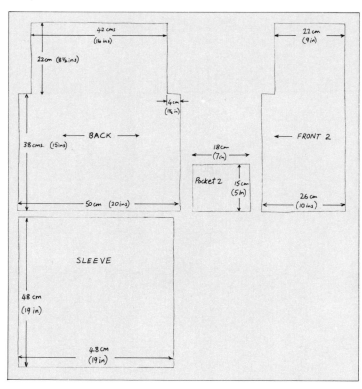

HANDKERCHIEF BORDER

VICTORIAN HANDKERCHIEF BAG

Here are two more examples of traditional crochet styles: an exquisite Victorian handkerchief bag in filet crochet and a pretty lacy edging for a fine cotton handkerchief. Filet work is a mesh fabric made by joining trebles [double crochet] with chain stitches. Patterns are formed by blocking in the spaces with stitches corresponding in number to the chains in the spaces. In the past this form of crochet was most often used for delicate lace curtains (see pattern for filet curtain, page 52) and for tablecloths. Today it is sometimes used for clothing also.

Handkerchief Border

MATERIALS

Yarn: 20 gm (¾ oz) of No. 80 (very fine) crochet cotton.

Linen or cotton handkerchief with hemmed edges.

1.00 mm [steel 10] crochet hook.

BRITISH PATTERN

1st round. Comm in corner, * 1 dc, 1 ch, rep from * to just before next corner, (1 dc, 1 ch) 3 times in corner, rep from beg on rem sides, ending with (1 dc, 1 ch) twice in corner, sl st in 1st dc, sl st back to previous ch sp.
Note. The number of chain spaces along each side of handkerchief should be a multiple of 7 plus 4.
2nd round. 1 dc in same ch sp, * 5 ch, miss 2 ch sps, 1 dc in next ch, (1 ch, 1 dc in next ch) 4 times, rep from * to 3rd last ch sp of 1st side. Turn corner, 5 ch, miss 2 ch sps, 1 dc in last ch of 1st side, 5 ch, 1 dc in 1st ch of next side, rep from * on rem sides, omitting last dc and ending with sl st on 1st dc, sl st in each of next 3 ch.
3rd round. 1 dc in same ch loop, * 4 ch, 1 dc in next ch sp, (1 ch, 1 dc in next ch) 3 times, 4 ch, 1 dc in 5 ch loop, rep from * to last loop before corner.
Turn corner, (4 ch, 1 dc in next loop) twice, rep from * on rem sides, omitting last dc and ending sl st in 1st dc, sl st in next ch.
4th round. 1 dc in same ch loop, * 4 ch, 1 dc in next ch sp, (1 ch, 1 dc in next ch) twice, 4 ch, 1 dc in 4 ch loop, rep from * up to last loop of 1st side. Turn corner, (4 ch, 1 dc in 4 ch loop, 1 ch, 1 dc in next loop) twice, rep from * on rem sides, omitting last dc and ending with sl st in 1st dc, sl st in next ch.
5th round. 1 dc in same ch loop * 4 ch, 1 dc in next ch sp, 1 ch, 1 dc in next ch sp, 4 ch, 1 dc in 4 ch loop, 1 ch, 1 dc in ch sp, 1 ch, 1 dc in 4 ch loop, rep from * up to last 4 ch loop before corner. Turn corner, 4 ch, 1 dc in 4 ch loop, (1 ch, 1 dc in next ch sp) twice, 4 ch, 1 dc in same loop, (1 ch, 1 dc in next ch sp) twice, rep from * on rem sides, omitting last dc and ending sl st

in 1st dc, sl st in next ch.
6th round. 1 dc in same ch loop, * 4 ch, 1 dc in next ch sp, 4 ch, 1 dc in 4 ch loop, (1 ch, 1 dc in next ch sp) twice, 1 ch, 1 dc in 4 ch loop, rep from * up to last 4 ch loop before corner.
Turn corner, ** 4 ch, 1 dc in 4 ch loop, (1 ch, 1 dc in next ch sp) 3 times, rep from ** once more, rep from * on rem sides, omitting last dc and ending sl st in 1st dc, sl st in next ch sp.
7th round. 1 dc in same ch loop, * 5 ch, 1 dc in next 4 ch loop, 1 ch, miss next ch sp, (1 tr, 1 ch) 5 times in next ch sp, miss next ch sp, 1 dc in 4 ch loop, rep from * to last 4 ch loop before corner. Turn corner, 2 dc in same loop, 1 ch, miss next ch sp, (1 tr, 1 ch) 5 times in next ch sp, miss next ch sp, ** 3 dc in next 4 ch loop, 1 ch, miss next ch sp, (1 tr, 1 ch) 5 times in next ch sp, rep from ** once, 1 dc in next 4 ch loop, rep from * on rem sides, omitting last dc and ending with sl st in 1st dc.
Fasten off.

AMERICAN PATTERN

1st round. Start in corner, * 1 sc, 1 ch, rep from * to just before next corner, (1 sc, 1 ch) 3 times in corner, rep from beg on remaining sides, ending with (1 sc, 1 ch) twice in corner, sl st in 1st sc, sl st back to previous ch sp.
Note. The number of chain spaces along each side of handkerchief should be a multiple of 7 plus 4.
2nd round. 1 sc in same ch sp, * 5 ch, skip 2 ch sps, 1 sc in next ch, (1 ch, 1 sc in next ch) 4 times, rep from * to 3rd last ch sp of 1st side. Turn corner, 5 ch, skip 2 ch sps, 1 sc in last ch of 1st side, 5 ch, 1 sc in 1st ch of next side, rep from * on remaining sides, omitting last sc and ending with sl st in 1st sc, sl st in each of next 3 ch.
3rd round. 1 sc in same ch loop, * 4 ch, 1 sc in next ch sp, (1 ch, 1 sc in next ch) 3 times, 4 ch, 1 sc in 5 ch loop, rep from * to last loop before corner. Turn corner, (4 ch, 1 sc in next loop) twice, rep from * on remaining sides, omitting last sc and ending sl st in 1st sc, sl st in next ch.

4th round. 1 sc in same ch loop * 4 ch, 1 sc in next ch sp (1 ch, 1 sc in next ch) twice, 4 ch, 1 sc in 4 ch loop, 1 ch, 1 sc in next 4 ch loop, rep from * up to last loop of 1st side. Turn corner, (4 ch, 1 sc in 4 ch loop, 1 ch, 1 sc in next loop) twice, rep from * on remaining sides, omitting last sc and ending with sl st in 1st sc, sl st in next ch.
5th round. 1 sc in same ch loop * 4 ch, 1 sc in next ch sp, 1 ch, 1 sc in next ch sp, 4 ch, 1 sc in 4 ch loop, 1 ch, 1 sc in ch sp, 1 ch, 1 sc in 4 ch loop, rep from * up to last 4 ch loop before corner. Turn corner, 4 ch, 1 sc in 4 ch loop, (1 ch, 1 sc in next ch sp) twice, 4 ch, 1 sc in same loop, (1 ch, 1 sc in next ch sp) twice, rep from * on remaining sides, omitting last sc and ending sl st in 1st sc, sl st in next ch.
6th round. 1 sc in same ch loop, * 4 ch, 1 sc in next ch sp, 4 ch, 1 sc in 4 ch loop, (1 ch, 1 sc in next ch sp) twice, 1 ch, 1 sc in 4 ch loop, rep from * up to last 4 ch loop before corner. Turn corner, ** 4 ch, 1 sc in 4 ch loop, (1 ch, 1 sc in next ch sp) 3 times, rep from ** once more, rep from * on remaining sides, omitting last sc and ending sl st in 1st sc, sl st in next ch sp.
7th round. 1 sc in same ch loop, * 5 ch, 1 sc in next 4 ch loop, 1 ch, skip next ch sp, (1 dc, 1 ch) 5 times in next ch sp, skip next ch sp, 1 sc in 4 ch loop, rep from * to last 4 ch loop before corner. Turn corner. 2 sc in same loop, 1 ch, skip next ch sp, (1 dc, 1 ch) 5 times in next ch sp, skip next ch sp, ** 3 sc in next 4 ch loop, 1 ch, skip next ch sp, (1 dc, 1 ch) 5 times in next ch sp, rep from ** once, 1 sc in next 4 ch loop, rep from * on remaining sides, omitting last sc and ending with sl st in 1st sc.
Fasten off.

Victorian Handkerchief Bag

Width: 32 cm (12½ in)
Depth: 24 cm (9½ in)

TENSION [GAUGE]

7 sps and 7 rows to 2.5 cm (1 in)

MATERIALS

Yarn: 40 gm (1½ oz) of No. 60 (fine) crochet cotton

2 m (2¼ yd) ribbon 1.5 cm (⅝ in) wide

60 cm (24 in) plastic strip 0.75 cm (¼ in) wide

0.60 mm [steel 14] crochet hook

BRITISH PATTERN

Front

Make 266 ch.
1st row. 1 tr into 8th ch from hook, * 2 ch, miss 2 ch, 1 tr in next ch, rep from * to end, 5 ch. Turn. (87 sp)

Foll chart from 2nd to 63rd row working 2 tr over 2 ch sp in each patt block, and turning with 5 ch at end of each row.
64th row. Miss 1st st, 1 dtr into next 3 sts, * 5 ch, miss 5 sts, 1 dtr into next 4 sts, rep from * ending 1 dtr in last st, 1 tr. Turn.
65th row. * 5 dc into 5 ch sp, 4 ch, miss 4 dtr, rep from * to end. Fasten off.

Back

Rejoin yarn to opposite side of foundation ch. Work 41 rows in ch sp. Foll chart from 42nd to 63rd row.
64th row. Work in sps, as 63rd row.
65th row. Work as 64th row of

Front, 9 ch. Turn.

66th row. Miss 1 dtr and 5 ch, * 1 dtr in next 4 dtr, 5 ch, rep from * ending with 4 dtr, 3 ch. Turn.

67th row. Miss 1st st, 1 tr in each st, to end.

Work 1 row dc along both side edges, working 3 dc in sp and 6 dc in deep sp. Fasten off.

Fold in half at foundation ch, noting back is higher than front. Starting at top edge join sides tog with dc, working through loops of back and front tog. Cont along fold, working 3 dc in each sp, and ending at top edge. Fasten off.

Comm at lower edge of one side, 1 dtr in 1st st, * 9 ch, miss 6 sts, 1 dtr in next st, rep from * up side, along back and down other side, working 1 dtr, 9 ch 1 dtr into corners, 1 ch. Turn.

Last row. * 9 dc in 9 ch loop, rep from * to end. Fasten off.

To finish: See American pattern

AMERICAN PATTERN
Front
Make 266 ch.

1st row. 1 dc into 8th ch from hook, * 2 ch, skip 2 ch, 1 dc in next ch, rep from * to end, 5 ch. Turn. (87 sp)

Follow chart from 2nd to 63rd row, working 2 dc over 2 ch sp in each pat block, and turning with 5 ch at end of each row.

64th row. Skip 1st st, 1 tr into next 3 sts, * 5 ch, skip 5 sts, 1 tr into next 4 sts, rep from * ending 1 tr in last st, 1 ch. Turn.

65th row. * 5 sc into 5 ch sp, 4 ch, skip 4 tr, rep from * to end. Fasten off.

Back
Rejoin yarn to opposite side of foundation ch. Work 41 rows in

ch sp. Follow chart from 42nd to 63rd row.

64th row. Work in sps, as 63rd row.

65th row. Work as 64th row of Front, 9 ch. Turn.

66th row. Skip 1 tr and 5 ch, * 1 tr in next 4 tr, 5 ch, rep from * ending with 4 tr, 3 ch. Turn.

67th row. Skip 1st st, 1 dc in each st to end.

Work 1 row sc along both side edges, working 3 sc in sp and 6 sc in deep sp. Fasten off.

Fold in half at foundation ch, noting back is higher than front. Starting at top edge, join sides tog with sc, working through loops of back and front tog. Continue along fold, working 3 sc in each sp, and ending at top edge. Fasten off.

Starting at lower edge of one side, 1 tr in 1st st, * 9 ch, skip 6 sts, 1 tr in next st, rep from * up

side, along back and down other side, working 1 tr, 9 ch, 1 tr into corners, 1 ch. Turn.

Last row. * 9 sc in 9 ch loop, rep from * to end. Fasten off.

To finish [BRITISH AND AMERICAN PATTERNS]
Cut 2 strips of plastic the same width as back, cover with ribbon and thread through sps at top of back. Cut another strip of plastic 5 cm (2 in) longer than back, cover with ribbon and thread through sps at front. Cut remaining ribbon in half, sew one piece to either end of front strip and tie in bow.

If you like, the bag can be lined with cotton or silk to show up the design.

☐ 1 space (2 ch., miss [skip] 2 sts. tr. [dc.] in next st)

☒ 1 block (3 tr. [3 dc.])

JACQUARD TOP
MOHAIR BED-JACKET

Two very different forms of crochet are explored in these two projects. The pretty jacquard top introduces the technique of changing yarn during the course of a row to create a pattern. The delicate openwork mohair bed-jacket is worked on hairpin prongs, a method described on page 31.

Jacquard Top

Bust/Chest: 76 (81, 86) cm
30 (32, 34) in
Length: 43.5 (45, 46.5) cm
17¼ (17¾, 18¼) in

TENSION [GAUGE]
14 sts to 10 cm (4 in) and 7 rows
tr [dc] to 9.5 cm (3¾ in) worked
on a 4.50 mm [G] hook.

MATERIALS
Yarn: 100 gm (4 oz) double
knitting (knitting
worsted) Colour A
(A = pink)
50 gm (2 oz) in Colour C, E
and G
(C, E, G = yellow, blue,
grey)
75 gm (3 oz) in Colour D
(D = brown)
25 gm (1 oz) in Colour B
and F
(B, F = green, purple)

**4.00 mm [F] and 4.50 mm [G]
crochet hooks**
Note: Each space on chart
represents 1 st. Shallow rows
are worked in dc [sc] and deep
rows in tr [dc].
Changing colour: Discard old
colour before last step of final st
in that colour, using new colour
to complete stitch. Do not cut
yarns temporarily not in use,
leave on wrong side of work.

BRITISH PATTERN
Back
With 4.50 mm hook and Col A
make 55 (59, 63) ch loosely.
1st row. (RS) 1 tr in 4th ch from
hook, 1 tr in each ch to end of
row. Turn. (53, 57, 61) sts)
Foll chart from Row 2.
Note: Neat ways of shaping
edges are described in Chapter 4.

Fronts
With 4.50 mm hook and Col A
make 4 ch loosely.
1st row. (F1 on chart) (WS) 1 dc
in 3rd ch from hook, 1 dc in next
ch. Turn. (3 sts)
2nd row. (F2 on chart) (RS) 3 ch
for 1st tr, 2 tr in 1st st, 1 tr in next
st, 3 tr in last st. Turn. (7 sts)
Foll chart from Row 3 (F3).

To make up
With right sides tog, join shoulders and side seams with backstitch.

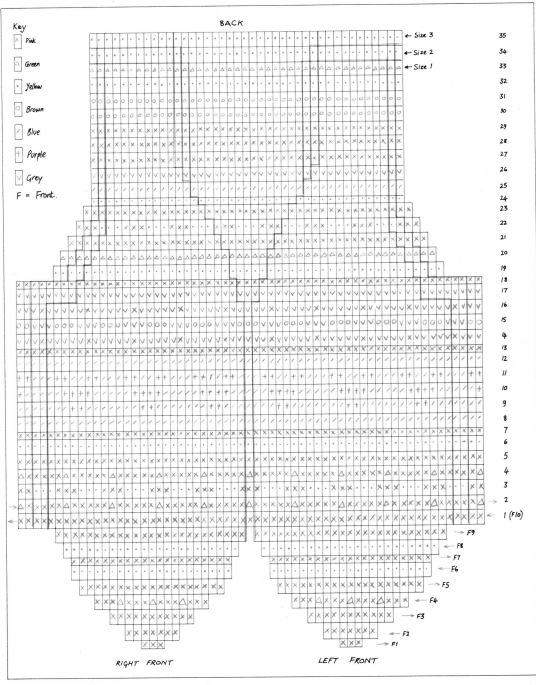

Key
X Pink
△ Green
· Yellow
○ Brown
/ Blue
+ Purple
∨ Grey

F = Front.

BACK

← Size 3   35
← Size 2   34
← Size 1   33
32
31
30
29
28
27
26
25
24
23
22
21
20
19
18
17
16
15
14
13
12
11
10
9
8
7
6
5
4
3
2
1 (F10)

→ F9
→ F8
→ F7
→ F6
→ F5
→ F4
→ F3
→ F2
→ F1

RIGHT FRONT   LEFT FRONT

Edging. With RS facing and
4.00 mm hook, join Col D to
armhole at side seam and work
3 rows dc around armhole
edge, joining each round with sl
st and dec at curve if necessary
to keep edging flat.
Rejoin Col D to lower edge of
back and work 2 rows dc round
entire outer edge of garment,
inc and dec as necessary.
Work 1 more row dc, marking
position of buttonhole loops on

right front and working thus:
7 ch, return over sts just
worked, miss 3 dc, sl st in next
dc, turn, 10 dc in 7 ch loop, sl st
in top of last dc in edging, cont
in dc, working 2 more buttonhole loops.

Buttons (make 3)
With 4.00 mm hook and Col D,
make 3 ch, sl st to form a ring.
1st round. 6 dc in ring, sl st to 1st
dc. (6 sts)

2nd round. 2 dc in each dc, sl st
to 1st dc. (12 sts)
3rd round. 1 dc in each dc, sl st
to 1st dc.
4th round. (dc 2 tog) 6 times all
round, sl st to 1st dc. (6 sts)
Stuff button firmly with padding
or spare yarn.
5th round. (dc 2 tog) 3 times, sl
st to 1st dc.
Fasten off leaving a thread to
draw up button. Sew on buttons
to correspond with loops.

AMERICAN PATTERN
Back
With Color A make 55 (59, 63) ch loosely.

1st row. (right side) 1 dc in 4th ch from hook, 1 dc in each ch to end of row. Turn. (53 (57, 61) sts)

Follow chart from Row 2.

Note. Ways of shaping edges are described in Chapter 4.

Fronts
With Color A make 4 ch loosely.

1st row. (F1 on chart) (wrong side) 1 sc in 3rd ch from hook, 1 sc in next ch. Turn. (3 sts)

2nd row. (F2 on chart) (right side) 3 ch for 1st dc, 2 dc in 1st st, 1 dc in next st.

3 dc in last st. Turn. (7 sts)

Follow chart from Row 3 (F3).

To finish
With right sides tog, join shoulder and side seams with backstitch.

Edging. With right side facing and size F hook, join Color D to armhole at side seam and work 3 rows sc around armhole edge, joining each round with sl st and dec at curve if necessary to keep edging flat. Rejoin Color D to lower edge of back and work 2 rows sc around entire outer edge of garment, inc and dec as necessary. Work 1 more row sc, marking position of buttonhole loops on right front and working this way: 7 ch return over sts just worked, skip 3 sc, sl st in next sc, turn, 10 sc in 7 ch loop, sl st in top of last sc in edging, continue in sc, working 2 more buttonhole loops.

Buttons (make 3)
With size F hook and Color D, make 3 ch, sl st to form a ring.

1st round. 6 sc in ring, sl st to 1st sc. (6 sts)

2nd round. 2 sc in each sc, sl st to 1st sc. (12 sts).

3rd round. 1 sc in each sc, sl st to 1st sc.

4th round. (sc 2 tog) 6 times all around, sl st to 1st sc. (6 sts) Stuff button firmly with padding or spare yarn.

5th round. (sc 2 tog) 3 times, sl st to 1st sc.

Fasten off leaving a thread to draw up button. Sew on buttons to correspond with loops.

Mohair Bed-jacket

Bust: 91/97 cm (36/38 in)

MATERIALS
Yarn: 300 gm (11 oz) [lightweight] mohair such as Emu Filigree

White shirring elastic

30 safety pins 2.5 cm (1 in)

Hairpin prong [fork], 80 mm (3 in) wide

7.00 mm [K] crochet hook

Note. Work all sts very loosely. To prevent strips twisting, pin loops tog in groups of 15.

BRITISH PATTERN
Body
With hairpin prong, and using Hairpin instructions with dc, make 4 strips with 195 loops on each side. Pin loops tog in grs of 15.

Edging row. Join loops along 1 edge of each strip, * 1 dc in 15 loops – 15 gr made – 3 ch (1 dc in 3 loops – 3 gr made, 3 ch) 5 times, rep from * along strip, ending 1 dc in 15 loops. Fasten off.

Join strips. Comm on free edge of 2nd strip. (1 dc in 3 loops, 3 ch) twice, 1 dtr in top of 15 gr on finished edge of 1st strip, sl st in 3 loops on 2nd strip, * (miss 1 ch, 1 dtr in next ch, 1 dtr in missed ch) twice, referred to as 2 dtr Cr, sl st to 3 loops on 2nd strip, rep from * once, 2 dtr Cr, 1 dc in 15 gr on 2nd strip.
** (2 dtr Cr, sl st to 3 loops on 2nd strip) 5 times, 2dtr Cr, 1 dc in 15 gr on 2nd strip, rep from ** to end, ending with (3 ch, sl st in 3 loops on 2nd strip) twice. Fasten off.

Join on 3rd and 4th strips in the same way. Each strip has 13 shell shapes.

Join sleeve. With 2 dtr Cr and sl st as before, work across first 4 shell shapes to join strip 1 to strip 4. Cont as for edging row across next 5 shell shapes of free edge of strip 1, then join strips with 2 dtr Cr over last 4 shell shapes. Fasten off.

Edging strip
Make strip with 180 loops on each side. Pin loops tog in 12 grs of 15 along 1 side. The other side is joined to the body in 36 grs of 5. Mark centre back of the jacket at lower edge (centre 3 grs of 5 in centre shell). Mark centre of edging strip, (space between 2 shells). Mark centre 3 grs of 2 centre shell shapes at upper edge for back of neck. With RS facing comm joining strip at left side of neck, 1 dc in gr on jacket, sl st to next 5 loops on strip, sl st in each 4 ch on jacket, sl st to next 5 loops on strip. Rep all round jacket, noting that at both sleeve joins, sl st to centre of 2 dtr Cr, and at centre back sl st in each ch, joining 5 loops to spaces between 3 loops on jacket and matching markers.

Outer edge of strip. * 1 dc in 15 gr, 3 ch, (1 dc, 1 ch, 1 dc) in spine between grs, 3 ch. Rep from * all round, dc across back neck. Work 2 rows in dc all round. Fasten off.

Cuffs
Comm at any dtr Cr on sleeve edge, with 3 dtr, * 1 dc in spine of next strip, 3 ch, 1 dc in each of 1st 4 ch on edge of same strip, 3 dtr in next dtr Cr, rep from * all round to straighten edge, sl st to 1st dtr.

Next row. 1 dc in each st, sl st to 1st dc. (approx 46 sts)

Next row. Dec by working 2 dcs tog all round, sl st to 1st dc. Work 2 more rounds in dc. Fasten off. Thread 2 rows of shirring elastic inside cuffs.

AMERICAN PATTERN
Body
With hairpin fork, and using Hairpin instructions with sc, make 4 strips with 195 loops on each side. Pin loops tog in groups of 15 to prevent twisting.

Edging row. Join loops along one edge of each strip, * 1 sc in 15 loops – 15 group made – 3 ch (1 sc in 3 loops – 3 group made – 3 ch) 5 times, rep from * along strip, ending 1 sc in 15 loops. Fasten off.

Join strips. Starting on free edge of 2nd strip, (1 sc in 3 loops, 3 ch) twice, 1 tr in top of 15 group on finished edge of 1st strip, sl st in 3 loops on 2nd strip, * (skip 1 ch, 1 tr in next ch, 1 tr in skipped ch) twice, referred to

as 2 tr Cr, sl st to 3 loops on 2nd strip, rep from * once, 2 tr Cr, 1 sc in 15 group on 2nd strip.
** (2 tr Cr, sl st to 3 loops on 2nd strip) 5 times, 2 tr Cr, 1 sc in 15 group on 2nd strip, rep from ** to end, ending with (3 ch, sl st in 3 loops on 2nd strip) twice. Fasten off. Join on 3rd and 4th strips in the same way.

Each strip has 13 shell shapes.

Join sleeve. With 2 tr Cr and sl st as before, work across first 4 shell shapes to join strip 1 to strip 4, cont as for edging row across next 5 shell shapes of free edge of strip 1, then join strips with 2 tr Cr over last 4 shell shapes. Fasten off.

Edging strip
Make strip with 180 loops on each side. Pin loops tog in 12 groups of 15 along one side. The other side is joined to the body in 36 groups of 5. Mark center back of jacket at lower edge (center 3 groups of 5 in center shell). Mark center of edging strip, (space between 2 shells). Mark center 3 groups of 2 center shell shapes at upper edge for back of neck. With right side facing start joining strip at left side of neck, 1 sc in group on jacket, sl st to next 5 loops on strip, sl st in each 4 ch on jacket, sl st to next 5 loops on strip. Rep all around jacket, noting that at both sleeve joinings, sl st to center of 2 tr Cr, and at center back sl st in each ch, joining 5 loops to spaces between 3 loops on jacket and matching markers.

Outer edge of strip. * 1 sc in 15 group, 3 ch, (1 sc, 1 ch, 1 sc) in spine between groups, 3 ch. Rep from * all around, sc across back neck. Work 2 rows in sc all around. Fasten off.

Cuffs
Start at any tr Cr on sleeve edge, with 3 tr, * 1 sc in spine of next strip, 3 ch, 1 sc in each of 1st 4 ch on edge of same strip, 3 tr in next tr Cr, rep from * all around to straighten edge, sl st to 1st tr.

Next row. 1 sc in each st, sl st to 1st sc. (approx 46 sts)

Next row. Dec by working 2 sc tog all around, sl st to 1st sc. Work 2 more rounds in sc. Fasten off. Thread 2 rows of shirring elastic inside cuffs.

SEAMLESS JACKET

This extremely versatile classic-styled jacket looks equally good over a smart blouse and skirt for town wear or with pullover and slacks for a day in the country. The subtle shading on the jacket is produced by changing one strand of colour only in every row. The combination and arrangement of colours are left to your personal choice, so no two jackets made up from these instructions will look exactly alike. You may like to introduce a wider range of toning colours to achieve an even greater variation of shading and texture – the possibilities are endless. However, care should be taken to maintain the same tension throughout.

Seamless Jacket

Bust: 91/96 cm (36/38 in)
Length: 61/63 cm (24/25 in)
Sleeve Seam: 41 cm (16 in)

TENSION [GAUGE]
6 V sts and 10 rows to 10 cm (4 in) over [in] patt worked on a 5.00 mm [H] hook, using 2 strands of yarn tog.

MATERIALS
Yarn: 110 gm (4 oz) 4 ply wool (Jacob) [sport yarn] in each of foll colours, Cream, Light Grey, Dark Grey, Marl.
80 (100) gm (3/4 oz) 4 ply wool (Llama) [sport yarn] in each of foll colours, Cream, Fawn, Brown, Charcoal, Grey.
Jacket illustrated was made in Ridgway House Farm 4 ply Jacob and Falcon Llama 4 ply. (see page 78 for suppliers)

5 buttons

5.00 mm [H] crochet hook.

Note. Use 2 different strands of yarn tog throughout (1 Jacob and 1 Llama). The shading is produced by changing one strand only on every row.

BRITISH PATTERN
Main Part
With 2 strands of yarn in selected colour, and 5.00 mm hook, comm at neck edge, make 53 ch.

1st row. 1 tr in 3rd ch from hook, * miss 1 ch, 2 tr in next ch, rep from * to end. (26 V sts)
Place coloured thread on 5th, 9th, 18th and 22nd V sts to mark position of raglan shaping.
2nd row. 3 ch (for 1st tr) 1 tr between 2 tr of previous row, * 2 tr between 2 tr of previous row, * rep from * to * twice, 4 tr between next 2 tr, rep from * to * across row, working 4 tr into each marked st. (30 V sts)
3rd, 5th and 7th rows. Work 1 V st in every V st.
4th row. Place coloured marker in 2nd and 3rd st of each inc gr. Patt to 1st marked st, work 2 V sts (4 tr) into each marked st, cont to end of row. (38 V sts)
6th row. Work in patt, inc 2 V sts at each point of raglan shaping. (46 V sts)
Cont to inc 8 V sts thus on every alt row until 94 (102) V sts are obtained. (18 (20) rows)
This completes yoke.
Divide for armholes.
Next row. Patt over 13 (14) V sts to centre of raglan shaping, miss 21 (23) V sts, patt over next 26 (28) V sts, miss 21 (23) V sts, patt to end. (52 (56) V sts). Cont straight in patt for 27 more rows. (46 (48) rows from neck). Fasten off.

Sleeves
Following the same colour sequence as for jacket from yoke downwards, join yarn between 2 V sts at underarm, 3 ch, 1 tr in same place, 1 V st in side of next V st, 1 V st in each of 21 (23) V sts left unworked, 1 V st in side of next V st, sl st to top of 3 ch to form round. Turn. (24 (26) V sts).
2nd round. 3 ch, 1 tr in underarm V st, patt to end, sl st into top of 3 ch. Turn. Work 6 more rounds as last round, turning at end of each round.
9th round. (1st dec) 3 ch, 1 tr in underarm V st, 1 tr in each of next 2 V sts, 1 V st in each V st to last 2 V sts, 1 tr in each of next V sts, sl st to top of 3 ch. Turn.
10th round. 3 ch, 1 tr in underarm V st, 1 V st between next 2 tr, patt to last 2 tr, 1 V st between 2 tr, sl st to top of 3 ch. Turn. (22 (24) V sts). Work 6 more rounds without further shaping.
17th round. (2nd dec) Dec 2 V sts as in 9th round. (20 (22) V sts). Work 7 rounds without shaping.
25th round. (3rd dec) Dec 2 V sts as 9th round. (18 (20) V sts). Work 7 rounds without shaping. (32 rounds from yoke)

For large size only, work 1 more dec round. (18 V sts)
Work 2nd sleeve in the same way.

Border
Using 2 strands of yarn, and with RS facing join yarn in last V st at lower edge of right front. 3 ch (for 1st tr) 1 tr in side of next V st on front edge, 2 tr in side of next V st, * (1 tr in side of next V st) twice, 2 tr in side of next V st, rep from * to neck edge, 4 tr in 1st V st at neck edge, 2 tr in each of next 24 V sts, 4 tr in last V st at neck edge, cont down left front as for right front, 4 tr in lower corner, 2 tr in every V st along lower edge, 3 tr in last V st, sl st to top of 3 ch. Turn.
2nd round. (WS facing) 1 ch, 1 dtr between 2 tr * 1 dc, 1 dtr between next 2 tr, rep from * 7 times more, ** 1 dc in next tr, 2 ch, miss 1 tr, (1 dc, 1 dtr between 2 tr) 4 times, rep from ** 3 times, 1 dc in next tr, 2 ch, miss 1 tr, 1 dc, 1 dtr between last 2 tr on right front (5 buttonholes worked) cont in patt to end of round, sl st to dc. Turn.
3rd round. 1 ch, 1 dtr in same place, 1 dc, 1 dtr in next dc, 2 dc, in 2 ch sp, 1 dc in dc, * 1 dc, 1 dtr in each of next 4 dc, 2 dc in 2 ch sp, 1 dc in dc. Rep from * 3 times. Cont 1 dc, 1 dtr in every foll dc all round, working 1 dc, 1 dtr in both sts at corners, sl st in 1 ch. Turn.
4th round. 1 ch, 1 dtr in same place, 1 dc, 1 dtr in next and every dc all round, sl st to 1 ch. Turn.
5th and 6th rounds. As 4th round. Fasten off.

Collar
Using 2 strands of yarn, and with RS facing, join yarn to 1st dc at neck edge of border, work 1 dc, 1 dtr patt across 30 grs. Work 2 more rows in patt. Cut yarn. Rejoin yarn in 6th row of neck border in dc immediately below point where 1st row of collar meets border, work 1 dc, 1 dtr patt all round collar ending in 6th row of border, 1 dc, 1 dtr in dc gr below collar. (32 grs). Cut yarn. Rejoin yarn in 1 dc of next gr in border below collar edging, 1 dc, 1 dtr in every dc round collar, ending 1 dc, 1 dtr in dc gr in border after 1st st of previous row. (34 grs). Fasten off.

Cuffs
Rejoin yarn in last round of sleeve. Work 9 rounds in 1 dc, 1 dtr patt (18 grs) changing colours as before, and turning at end of each round. Fasten off. Turn back cuffs. Sew on buttons to correspond with buttonholes.

AMERICAN PATTERN
Main Part
With 2 strands of yarn in selected color, and size H hook, starting at neck edge, make 53 ch.

1st row. 1 dc in 3rd ch from hook, * skip 1 ch, 2 dc in next ch, rep from * to end. (26 V sts)
Place colored thread on 5th, 9th, 18th and 22nd V sts to mark position of raglan shaping.
2nd row. 3 ch (for 1st dc) 1 dc between 2 dc of previous row, * 2 dc between 2 dc of previous row, * rep from * to * twice, 4 dc between next 2 dc, rep from * to * across row, working 4 dc into each marked st. (30 V sts)
3rd, 5th and 7th rows. Work 1 V st in every V st.
4th row. Place colored marker in 2nd and 3rd st of each inc group. Pat to 1st marked st, work 2 V sts (4 dc) into each marked st, continue to end of row. (38 V sts)
6th row. Work in pat, inc 2 V st at each point of raglan shaping. (46 V sts)
Continue to inc 8 V sts this way on every other row until 94 (102) V sts are obtained. (18 (20) rows). This completes yoke.
Divide for armholes.
Next row. Pat over 13 (14) V sts to center of raglan shaping, skip 21 (23) V sts, pat over next 26 (28) V sts, skip 21 (23) V sts,

pat to end. (52 (56) V sts).
Continue straight in pat for 27
more rows. (46 (48) rows from
neck). Fasten off.

Sleeves
Following the same color sequence as for jacket from yoke
downwards, join yarn between
2 V sts at underarm, 3 ch, 1 dc in
same place, 1 V st in side of next
V st, 1 V st in each of next 21 (23)
V sts left unworked, 1 V st in
side of next V st, sl st to top of
3 ch to form round. Turn. (24
(26) V sts)
2nd round. 3 ch, 1 dc in underarm V st, pat to end, sl st into top
of 3 ch. Turn. Work 6 more
rounds as last rnd, turning at
end of each round.
9th round. (1st dec) 3 ch, 1 dc in
underarm V st, 1 dc in each of
next 2 V sts, 1 V st in each V st to
last 2 V sts, 1 dc in each of next V
sts, sl st to top of 3 ch. Turn.
10th round. 3 ch, 1 dc in underarm V st, 1 V st between next
2 dc, pat to last 2 dc, 1 V st
between 2 dc, sl st to top of 3 ch.
Turn. (22 (24) V sts). Work 6
more rounds without further
shaping.
17th round. (2nd dec) Dec 2 V
sts as in 9th round. (20 (22) V
sts). Work 7 rounds without
shaping.
25th round. (3rd dec) Dec 2 V
sts as 9th round. (18 (20) V sts).
Work 7 rounds without shaping.
(32 rounds from yoke)
For large size only, work 1 more
dec round (18 V sts)
Work 2nd sleeve in the same
way.

Border
Using 2 strands of yarn, and
with right side facing join yarn
in last V st at lower edge of right
front. 3 ch (for 1st dc) 1 dc in
side of next V st on front edge,
2 dc in side of next V st, * (1 dc in
side of next V st) twice, 2 dc in
side of next V st, rep from * to
neck edge, 4 dc in 1st V st at
neck edge, 2 dc in each of next
24 V sts, 4 dc in last V st at neck
edge, continue down left front
as for right front, 4 dc in lower
corner, 2 dc in every V st along
lower edge, 3 dc in last V st, sl st
to top of 3 ch. Turn.
2nd round. (Wrong side facing)
1 ch, 1 tr between 2 dc, * 1 sc,
1 tr between next 2 dc, rep from
* 7 times more, ** 1 sc in next

dc, 2 ch, skip 1 dc, (1 sc, 1 tr
between 2 dc) 4 times, rep from
** 3 times, 1 sc in next dc, 2 ch,
skip 1 dc, 1 sc, 1 tr between last
2 dc on right front (5 buttonholes worked) continue in pat
to end of round, sl st to sc. Turn.
3rd round. 1 ch, 1 tr in same
place, 1 sc, 1 tr in next sc, 2 sc in
2 ch sp, 1 sc in sc, * 1 sc, 1 tr in
each of next 4 sc, 2 sc in 2 ch sp,
1 sc in sc. Rep from * 3 times.
Continue 1 sc, 1 tr in every foll
sc all around, working 1 sc, 1 tr
in both sts at corners, sl st in
1 ch. Turn.
4th round. 1 ch, 1 tr in same
place, 1 sc, 1 tr in next and
every sc all around, sl st to 1 ch.
Turn.
5th and 6th rounds. As 4th
round. Fasten off.

Collar
Using 2 strands of yarn, and
with right side facing, join yarn
to 1st sc at neck edge of border,
work 1 sc, 1 tr pat across
30 groups. Work 2 more rows in
pat. Cut yarn. Rejoin yarn in 6th
row of neck border in sc immediately below point where
1st row of collar meets border,
work 1 sc, 1 tr pat all around
collar ending in 6th row of
border, 1 sc, 1 tr in sc group
below collar. (32 groups). Cut
yarn.
Rejoin yarn in 1 sc of next group
in border below collar edging,
1 sc, 1 tr in every sc around
collar, ending 1 sc, 1 tr in sc
group in border after 1st st of
previous row. (34 groups).
Fasten off.

Cuffs
Rejoin yarn to last round of
sleeve. Work 9 rounds in 1 sc,
1 tr pat (18 groups) changing
colors as before, and turning at
end of each round. Fasten off.
Turn back cuffs. Sew on buttons
to correspond with buttonholes.

FLOWER BASKET BEDSPREAD

This lovely crocheted bedspread involves a lot of work, but is well worth the effort.

Width: 180 cm (71 in)
Length: 270 cm (106 in)
(excluding border)

TENSION [GAUGE]
Square measures approx 30 cm (12 in)

MATERIALS
Yarn: 2800 gm (100 oz) double
knitting [knitting
worsted] yarn in White
450 gm (17 oz) in Blue
450 gm (17 oz) in Green
150 gm (6 oz) in Pink

4.00 mm [F] crochet hook

BRITISH PATTERN
Motif
With white yarn, make 40 ch.
1st row. 1 dc in 2nd ch from hook, 1 dc in each ch to end. (39 sts). Each square on diagram represents 1 dc. Follow diagram below – and individual patterns on page 72 – joining colours into last st before new colour is required, and leaving ends of yarn on wrong side of work. Colours can be carried loosely and woven in if preferred. Cont until diagram is completed. Fasten off.

Edging
1st round. Work in dc, with 37 sts on each side of square, and 3 sts in each corner.

2nd round. Yrh, insert hook in next st, yrh, pull loop through, yrh, insert hook into same st, yrh, pull loop through, yrh, pull through all loops (1 bobble) * 1 ch, miss 1 dc, 1 bobble in next dc, rep from * all around square, working 1 bobble into each of 3 sts at corners.
3rd round. As 2nd round, working bobbles into ch sp and 1 bobble in centre bobble at corners. Fasten off.
Make 14 squares following diagrams 1 and 2, and 13 squares following diagrams 3 and 4. (54 squares)
Sew or crochet the squares together following the numbered diagram.

Peaked border
(2 peaks to each square)
Join yarn at corner of square.
1st row. * 1 bobble, 1 ch, rep from * 10 times. (11 bobbles). Turn.
Cont working bobbles into ch sp. (10 bobbles). Dec 1 bobble on each row until 3 bobbles rem.
Next row. 2 ch, 1 bobble in centre bobble, 2 ch, sl st in last bobble of previous row. Fasten off.
Work 2nd peak in the same way, starting in next sp on square. Rep border all round bedspread.

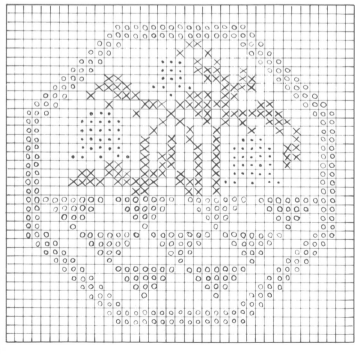

AMERICAN PATTERN
Motif
With white yarn, make 40 ch.
1st row. 1 sc in 2nd ch from hook, 1 sc in each ch to end. (39 sts)

Each square on diagram represents 1 sc. Follow diagram on previous page and the individual patterns below, joining colors into last st before new color is required, and leaving ends of yarn on wrong side of work, to be darned in later. Colors can be carried loosely and woven in if preferred. Cont until diagram is completed. Fasten off.

Edging
1st round. Work in sc, with 37 sts on each side of square, and 3 sts in each corner.
2nd round. Yo, insert hook in next st, yo, draw loop through, yo, insert hook in same st, yo, draw loop through, yo, draw through all loops (1 bobble) * 1 ch, skip 1 sc, 1 bobble in next sc, rep from * all around square, working 1 bobble into each of 3 sts at corners.

3rd round. As 2nd round, working bobbles into ch sp and 1 bobble in center bobble at corners. Fasten off.

Make 14 squares following diagrams 1 and 2, and 13 squares following diagrams 3 and 4. (54 squares)

Sew or crochet squares together following the numbered diagram.

Peaked border
(2 peaks to each square)
Join yarn at corner of square.
1st row. * 1 bobble, 1 ch, rep from * 10 times. (11 bobbles). Turn.

Continue working bobbles into ch sp. (10 bobbles). Dec 1 bobble on each row until 3 bobbles rem.

Next row. 2 ch, 1 bobble in center bobble, 2 ch, sl st in last bobble of previous row. Fasten off.

Work 2nd peak in the same way, starting in next sp on square. Rep border all around bedspread.

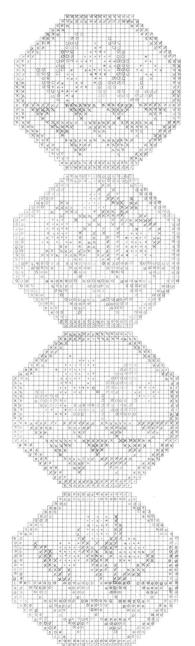

Oversweater

Bust: 96 cm (38 in)
Length: 67 cm (26½ in)
Sleeve Seam: 41 cm (16 in)

TENSION [GAUGE]
18 sts and 17 rows to 10 cm (4 in) worked over [in] trellis patt with a 3.50 mm [E] hook.

MATERIALS
Yarn: 910 gm (32 oz) 4 ply wool such as Ridgway House Farm Jacob 4 ply. [2 ply sport weight yarn] (see page 78 for suppliers).

3.50 mm [E] crochet hook.

BRITISH PATTERN
Basic border pattern
1st row. (RS) Work in dc. Do not turn.
2nd row. (RS) Work in dc into FRONT loop only. i.e. corded edge. Do not turn.
3rd row. (RS) Work in dc into BACK loop only of 1st row. Turn.
4th row. (WS) Work in dc into both loops, normally with 1 bobble into every 4th st. Turn.

Front and back centre panels (make 2)
Make 26 ch.
1st row. 1 tr in 4th ch from hook, 1 tr in every ch to end of row. (24 tr)
2nd row. (RS) 1 ch (does not count as 1st st) 1 dc in 1st st, yrh twice, insert hook in 4th ch of base ch, bringing hook down in front of tr row, (yrh, draw through 2 loops) twice – called open dtr. Insert hook in next tr, draw loop through, yrh, draw through 3 loops on hook, * 1 dc in each of next 2 tr, 1 open dtr in same (4th) base ch, miss next 2 ch, 1 open dtr in next base ch, insert hook in next tr, draw loop through, yrh, draw through 4 loops on hook.
Rep from * to last 4 sts, 1 dc in each of next 2 tr, 1 open dtr in same place as last dtr, insert hook in next tr, draw loop through, yrh and draw through 3 loops on hook, 1 dc in turning ch. (7 raised V sts). Turn.
3rd and 5th rows. 3 ch (for 1st tr) miss 1st st, 1 tr in next and every foll st to end of row. Turn. (24 tr)
4th row. 1 ch (does not count as 1st st) 1 dc in 1st and each of

next 2 tr, * 1 open dtr under stem of 1st dtr in 2nd row, inserting hook from right to left behind st, 1 open dtr under both sts of next 2 dtr gr, insert hook in next tr, draw loop through, yrh, draw through 4 loops on hook, 1 dc in each of next 2 tr, rep from * to end. Turn.
6th row. Work as 2nd row, but inserting hook under 2 dtr gr in 4th row.
Last 4 rows form Raised Trellis patt. Cont until panel measures 54 cm (21¼ in).
Fasten off.
Make 2nd panel in same way.

Centre panel borders
Comm at top left corner, RS facing, join yarn to last st of last row.
Work Border patt rows 1–4 once, and rows 1–3 again.
Note: On 1st row work 1 dc into each row and into base ch. Work a similar border on right side of panel, joining yarn in base ch in lower right corner. Rep borders on each side of 2nd panel. Panel measures 54 × 18 cm (24¼ × 7⅛ in).

'Daisy' panels (make 4)
Daisy
Make 3 ch and sl st to form a ring.
1st round. 2 ch (for 1st dc) 7 dc in ring join with sl st to top of 2 ch. (8 sts)
2nd round. 3 ch (for 1st tr) * wind yarn 10 times round hook, insert hook in next dc, draw loop through (12 loops on hook) yrh, draw yarn through 2 loops (11 loops on hook), using forefinger and thumb of left hand, pass last 10 loops evenly over 1st loop (loop nearest barb on hook) extending this loop as you proceed to height of 3 ch, yrh, without tightening, draw through top of long loop which forms core of st (1 bullion st, 10 loops must lie evenly and close tog to form neat column). 1 tr in same dc, rep from * 6 times, work 1 bullion st in st at beg of round, immediately in front of 3 ch, sl st to top of 3 ch.

3rd round. 1 ch (for 1st st) * dc under top 2 loops of st at right of bullion st, 1 dc in sp between column of bullion st and thread to left of it, 1 dc in next tr, rep from * 7 times, omitting 1 dc in 1 tr at end of last rep, sl st in 1 ch. (24 dc)
Fasten off. Leave length of yarn for joining.
Make 44 Daisies in all, 11 for each panel. Join Daisies tog with free end of yarn, stitching 4 sts at each side tog, leaving 8 sts free on each side.

Daisy panel borders
With RS of Daisy panel facing, count 9 sts back from join in 1st and 2nd Daisies and join yarn into this st. (See diagram.)
1st row. (RS) 3 ch (for 1st tr), 1 tr in same place, miss next st, * sl st into each of next 6 sts, miss next st, 3 tr into join between Daisies, miss next st on next Daisy, rep from * to last Daisy, sl st into each of next 6 sts, miss next st, 2 tr in next st. Fasten off. Do not turn.
Rejoin yarn to top of 3 ch at beg of 1st row.
2nd, 3rd and 4th rows. Work Border patt rows 1–3. Fasten off. Rep from beg of Daisy panel border along other edge. Do not fasten off, cont.
5th to 11th rows. Work Border patt rows 1–4 once, and then rows 1–3 again.
Panel of 11 Daisies after completion of borders measures 54 × 10 cm (21¼ × 4 in).
Make 3 more panels in the same way.
Place 1 Daisy panel on each side of centre panel, wide borders to the outside, narrow borders side by side border of centre panel. Using flat seam join tog. Each 3 panel section measures 54 × 38 cm (21¼ × 15 in).

Shoulder border (worked on each 3 panel section)
Right shoulder
With RS facing, join yarn in last st of wide border of righthand Daisy panel.
1st row. 1 ch (for 1st dc) 4 dc in edge sts of border, 11 sts in edge sts of Daisy panel, 5 dc in edge sts of narrow border, join and last row of centre panel border. (21 dc)
2nd to 10th rows. Work Border patt rows 2–3, then 1–4, and 1–3 again.
Left shoulder
Join yarn in edge st of last row of lefthand centre panel border. Cont as for right shoulder border. When borders have been worked on both 3 panel sections, join at shoulders, RS facing, using flat seam.

Neck border
With RS facing, join yarn in top righthand corner of centre panel, dc across 24 sts, * 3 dc, 2 dc tog in edge sts of centre panel border, 1 dc in corner, 2 dc tog, 6 dc in edge sts of 1st shoulder border, 6 dc, 2 dc tog in edge sts of 2nd border, 1 dc in corner, 2 dc tog, 3 dc in centre panel border * 24 dc across centre panel. Rep from * to * sl st in 1st ch. (96 sts)
2nd round. (RS) Work Border patt row 2.
3rd round. Work Border patt row 3, but working 2 dc tog before and after each corner. (88 sts)
4th round. Work Border patt row 4.
5th round. Work Border patt row 5, but dec as before. (80 sts)
6th round. Work corded edge, inserting hook through BOTH loops of each st. Fasten off.

Pattern continued on page 76.

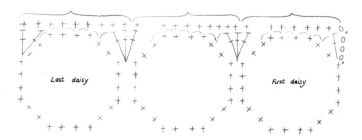

Last daisy   First daisy

OVERSWEATER

The intricate patterns of this handsome over-sweater are reminiscent of Aran knitting and are shown to full advantage by the natural-coloured yarn. Equally wearable by men and women, it's just the thing for a day's sailing – pondside or seaside variety. But it's definitely a project for the experienced crocheter. Instructions begin on page 73 and continue on the following pages.

Side (underarm) panel (make 2)
Make 14 ch.
Work in Raised Trellis patt as centre panels (12 tr) until work measures 37 cm (14½ in). Fasten off.

Sleeve panel (make 2 for each sleeve)
Make 32 ch.
Work in Raised Trellis patt as centre panels (30 tr) until work measures 41 cm (16 in), mark edges of work with coloured thread, then work another 6 rows in patt. Fasten off.
Make 3 more panels in the same way.
Sew 2 sleeve panels tog along long edges from base row to coloured thread markers (underarm seam).
Sew rem section of Sleeve panel to top edge of side panel, with underarm seam to centre of side panel.

Side and sleeve panel border
With RS facing, work border on long side of Side panel, cont over end of Sleeve panel.
1st to 3rd rows. Work Border patt rows 1–3 once.
4th and 5th rows. Rep last 2 rows once.
Rep this border on other side of Side/Sleeve panel and on both sides of 2nd Side/Sleeve panel.

Sleeve panel border (between wrist and shoulder)
Work border over rem long edge of all Sleeve panels.
1st to 3rd rows. Work Border patt rows 1–3.
4th to 6th rows. Work Border patt rows 2–4.
7th to 9th rows. Work Border patt rows 1–3.
Fasten off.
Join sleeve and side panel section to main body panels from lower edge to shoulder border.
Join sleeves from wrist to shoulder.

Cuffs
With RS facing, work 1 row dc evenly around lower edge of each sleeve, joining with sl st. Turn and work 1 row dc, dec evenly if necessary to obtain 65 sts in round.
Make 8 Daisies for each cuff.
Join into ring as for Daisy panel, then work borders round

upper and lower edges, joining rounds with sl st.
1st round. Work as for Daisy panel border 1st row.
2nd to 5th rounds. Work Border patt rows 1–4.
6th to 8th rounds. Work Border patt rows 1–3.
9th round. (Worked on lower edge only.) Work corded edge through BOTH loops.
Sew border of cuff (with 8 rounds) to lower edge of sleeve, making sure that RS of cuff will appear on outside when cuff is turned back.

Border at lower edge of sweater
1st round. With RS facing, work in dc evenly round lower edge of sweater, sl st to 1st dc.
Do not turn. (Approx. 184 sts)
2nd to 4th rounds. Work Border patt rows 2–4.
5th round. Work Border patt row 1, dec evenly to leave 176 sts.
6th and 7th rounds. Work Border patt rows 2–3.
Fasten off.
Make 20 Daisies. Sew tog to form a ring as before.

Upper edge
1st round. Work as for Daisy panel border 1st row. (160 sts)
2nd and 3rd rounds. Work Border patt row 1–2.
4th round. Work Border patt row 3, but work 2 dc into every 10th st 16 times. (176 sts)
Fasten off.

Lower edge
1st to 4th rounds. As for upper edge but without increasing. (160 sts)
5th round. Work Border patt row 4.
6th to 8th rounds. Work Border patt rows 1–3.
9th round. Work corded edge under BOTH loops. Fasten off.

AMERICAN PATTERN
Basic border pattern
1st row. (Right side) Work in sc. Do not turn.
2nd row. (Right side) Work in sc into FRONT loop only, i.e. corded edge. Do not turn.
3rd row. (Right side) Work in sc into BACK loop only of 1st row. Turn.
4th row. (Wrong side) Work in sc into both loops, normally with 1 bobble into every 4th st. Turn.

Front and back center panels (make 2)
Make 26 ch.
1st row. 1 dc in 4th ch from hook, 1 dc in every ch to end of row. (24 dc)
2nd row. (Right side) 1 ch (does not count as 1st st) 1 sc in 1st st, yo twice, insert hook in 4th ch of base ch, bringing hook down in front of dc row, (yo, draw through 2 loops) twice – called open tr. Insert hook in next dc, draw loop through, yo, draw through 3 loops on hook, * 1 sc in each of next 2 dc, 1 open tr in same (4th) base ch, skip next

2 ch, 1 open tr in next base ch, insert hook in next dc, draw loop through, yo, draw through 4 loops on hook. Rep from * to last 4 sts, 1 sc in each of next 2 dc, 1 open tr in same place as last tr, insert hook in next dc, draw loop through, yo and draw through 3 loops on hook, 1 sc in turning ch. (7 raised V sts). Turn.
3rd and 5th rows. 3 ch (for 1st dc) skip 1st st, 1 dc in next and every following st to end of row. Turn. (24 dc)
4th row. 1 ch (does not count as 1st st) 1 sc in 1st and each of next 2 dc, * 1 open tr under stem of 1st tr in 2nd row, inserting hook from right to left behind st, 1 open tr under both sts of next 2 tr group, insert hook in next dc, draw loop through, yo, draw through 4 loops on hook, 1 sc in each of next 2 dc, rep from * to end. Turn.
6th row. Work as 2nd row, but inserting hook under 2 tr group in 4th row.
Last 4 rows form Raised Trellis pat. Continue until panel measures 54 cm (21¼ in). Fasten off. Make 2nd panel the same way.

Center panel borders
Start at top left corner, right side facing, join yarn to last st of last row.
Work Border pat rows 1–4 once, and rows 1–3 again.
Note. On 1st row work 1 sc into each row and into base ch.

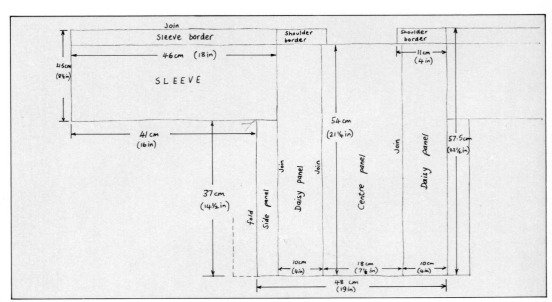

Work a similar border on right side of panel, joining yarn in base ch in lower right corner. Rep borders on each side of 2nd panel.
Panel measures 54 × 18 cm (21¼ × 7⅛ in)

'Daisy' panels (make 4)
Daisy
Make 3 ch and sl st to form a ring.
1st round. 2 ch (for 1st sc) 7 sc in ring, join with sl st to top of 2 ch. (8 sts)
2nd round. 3 ch (for 1st dc) * wind yarn 10 times around hook, insert hook in next sc, draw loop through (12 loops on hook) yo, draw yarn through 2 loops (11 loops on hook), using forefinger and thumb of left hand, pass last 10 loops evenly over 1st loop (loop nearest hook) extending this loop as you proceed to height of 3 ch, yo, without tightening, draw through top of long loop which forms core of st (1 bullion st, 10 loops must lie evenly and close tog to form neat column). 1 dc in same sc, rep from * 6 times, work 1 bullion st in st at beg of round, immediately in front of 3 ch, sl st to top of 3 ch.
3rd round. 1 ch (for 1st st) * sc under top 2 loops of st at right of bullion st, 1 sc in sp between column of bullion st and thread to left of it, 1 sc in next dc, rep from * 7 times, omitting 1 sc in 1 dc at end of last rep, sl st in 1 ch. (24 sc)
Fasten off. Leave length of yarn for joining.
Make 44 Daisies in all, 11 for each panel.
Join Daisies tog with free end of yarn, stitching 4 sts at each side tog, leaving 8 sts free on each side.

Daisy panel border
With right side of Daisy panel facing, count 9 sts back from joining in 1st and 2nd Daisies and join yarn at this st. (See diagram.)
1st row. (right side) 3 ch (for 1st dc) 1 dc in same place, skip next st, * sl st into each of next 6 sts, skip next st, 3 dc into joining between Daisies, skip next st on next Daisy, rep from * to last Daisy, sl st into each of next 6 sts, skip next st, 2 dc in next st. Fasten off. Do not turn.

Rejoin yarn to top of 3 ch at beg of 1st row.
2nd, 3rd and 4th rows. Work Border pat rows 1–3. Fasten off. Rep from beg of Daisy panel border along other edge. Do not fasten off, continue.
5th to 11th rows. Work Border pat rows 1–4 once, and then rows 1–3 again.
Panel of 11 Daisies after completion of borders measures 21¼ × 4 in.
Make 3 more panels in the same way.
Place 1 Daisy panel on each side of center panel, wide borders to the outside, narrow borders side by side border of center panel. Using flat seam join tog. Each 3 panel section measures 21¼ × 15 in.

Shoulder border (worked on each 3 panel section)
Right shoulder
With right side facing, join yarn in last st of wide border of right-hand Daisy panel.
1 ch (for 1st sc) 4 sc in edge sts of border, 11 sts in edge sts of Daisy panel, 5 sc in edge sts of narrow border, join and last row of center panel border. (21 sc)
2nd to 10th rows. Work Border pat rows 2–3, then 1–4, and 1–3 again.
Left shoulder
Join yarn in edge st of last row of lefthand center panel border. Continue as for right shoulder border. When borders have been worked on both 3 panel sections, join at shoulders, right sides facing, using flat seam.

Neck border
With right side facing, join yarn in top righthand corner of center panel, sc across 24 sts, * 3 sc, 2 sc tog in edge sts of center panel border, 1 sc in corner, 2 sc tog, 6 sc in edge sts of 1st shoulder border, 6 sc, 2 sc tog in edge sts of 2nd border, 1 sc in corner, 2 sc tog, 3 sc in center panel border * 24 sc across center panel. Rep from * to * sl st in 1st ch. (96 sts)
2nd round. (right side) Work Border pat row 2.
3rd round. Work Border pat row 3, but working 2 sc tog before and after each corner. (88 sts)

4th round. Work Border pat row 4.
5th round. Work Border pat row 5, but dec as before. (80 sts)
6th round. Work in corded edge, inserting hook through BOTH loops of each st. Fasten off.

Side (underarm) panel (make 2)
Make 14 ch.
Work in Raised Trellis pat as center panel (12 dc) until work measures 37 cm (14½ in). Fasten off.

Sleeve panel (make 2 for each sleeve)
Make 32 ch.
Work in Raised Trellis pat as center panels (30 dc) until work measures 41 cm (16 in). Mark edges of work with colored thread, then work another 6 rows in pat. Fasten off.
Make 3 more panels in the same way.
Sew 2 sleeve panels tog along long edges from base row to colored thread markers. (Underarm seam).
Sew remaining section of Sleeve panel to top edge of Side panel, with underarm seam to center of side panel.

Side and sleeve panel border
With right side facing, work border on long side of Side panel, continue over end of Sleeve panel.
1st to 3rd rows. Work Border pat rows 1–3 once.
4th and 5th rows. Rep last 2 rows once.
Rep this border on other side of Side/Sleeve panel and on both sides of 2nd Side/Sleeve panel.
Sleeve panel border (between wrist and shoulder)
Work border over remaining long edge of all Sleeve panels.
1st to 3rd rows. Work Border pat rows 1–3.
4th to 6th rows. Work Border pat rows 2–4.
7th to 9th rows. Work Border pat rows 1–3.
Fasten off.
Join sleeve and side panel section to main body panels from lower edge to shoulder border.
Join sleeves from wrist to shoulder.

Cuffs
With right side facing work 1 row sc evenly around lower edge of each sleeve, joining with sl st.
Turn and work 1 row sc, dec evenly if necessary to obtain 65 sts in round.
Make 8 Daisies for each cuff. Join into ring as for Daisy panel, then work borders around upper and lower edges, joining rounds with sl st.
1st round. Work as for Daisy panel border 1st row.
2nd to 5th rounds. Work Border pat rows 1–4.
6th to 8th rounds. Work Border pat rows 1–3.
9th round. (Worked on lower edge only). Work corded edge through BOTH loops.
Sew border of cuff (with 8 rounds) to lower edge of sleeve, making sure that right side of cuff will appear on outside when cuff is turned back.

Border at lower edge of sweater
1st round. With right side facing, work in sc evenly around lower edge of sweater, sl st to 1st sc. Do not turn. (Approx 184 sts)
2nd to 4th rounds. Work Border pat rows 2–4.
5th round. Work Border pat row 1, dec evenly to leave 176 sts.
6th and 7th rounds. Work Border pat rows 2–3.
Fasten off.
Make 20 Daisies. Sew tog to form a ring as before.
Upper edge
1st round. Work as for Daisy panel border 1st row. (160 sts)
2nd and 3rd rounds. Work Border pat row 1–2.
4th round. Work Border pat row 3, but work 2 sc into every 10th st 16 times (176 sts). Fasten off.
Lower edge
1st to 4th rounds. As for upper edge but without increasing. (160 sts)
5th round. Work Border pat row 4.
6th to 8th rounds. Work Border pat rows 1–3.
9th round. Work corded edge under BOTH loops.
Fasten off.

Crochet Supplies

UNITED KINGDOM

The yarns used for the projects on pages 66 and 74 are obtainable from the following:

Ridgeway House Farm
Runwick
Farnham
Surrey

R S Duncan & Co
Falcon Mills
Bartle Lane
Bradford
W Yorks

The following sell hooks and/or yarns by mail order:

The Silver Thimble
33 Gay Street
Bath
Avon BA1 2NT
Tel: Bath 23457
hooks and yarns

William Hall & Co (Monsall) Ltd
177 Stanley Road
Cheadle Hulme
Cheadle
Cheshire SK8 6RF
fancy yarns

Ries Wools of Holborn
242/243 High Holborn
London WC1
Tel: 01 242 7721
hooks and yarns

Texere Yarns
College Mill
Barkerend Road
Bradford
W Yorks BD3 9AQ
Tel: Bradford 22191
wide selection of yarns

Patricia Roberts Knitting Shop
60 Kinnerton Street
London SW1
Tel: 01 235 4742
yarns

A K Graupner
Corner House
Valley Road
Bradford
W Yorks BD1 4AA
yarns

Craftsman's Mark Yarn Ltd
Trefnant
Welshpool
Powys
N Wales LL16 5UD
natural yarns

Other useful addresses:

Spinning and Equipment

British Wool Marketing Board
Oak Mills
Station Road
Clayton
Bradford
W Yorks BD14 6JD
Tel: Bradford 882091
fleece

Handweavers Studio and Gallery Ltd
29 Haroldstone Road
London E17 7AN
general equipment

Eliza Leadbeater
Rookery Cottage
Whitegate
Nr Northwich
Cheshire TW8 2BN
yarns and spinning wheels

Dyeing

Muswell Hill Weavers
65 Rosebery Road
London N10 2LE
Russell dye system

Mateson Dyes & Chemicals
Marcon Place
London E8 1LP
natural dyes and mordants

Guilds

Knitting and Crochet Guild
80 Stoneleigh Street
Derker
Oldham
Lancs OL1 4LD
Mrs L S Mills (Secretary)

Association of Guilds of Spinners, Weavers and Dyers
c/o The Federation of British Craft Societies
80a Southampton Row
London WC1 4BA

UNITED STATES

The following nationwide chain stores usually stock a wide selection of crochet supplies: **Ben Franklin Stores; Jefferson Stores; Kay Mart; M H Lamston; The May Co; Neisners; J C Penney Stores; Sears Roebuck; Two Guys** and **Woolworth's.**

The following sell crochet supplies by mail order:

American Handicrafts
2617 W Seventh Street
Fort Worth, Texas 76707

Lee Wards
Elgin, Illinois 60120

Peters Valley Craftsmen
Layton, New Jersey 07851

Economy Handicrafts
50–21 69th Street
Woodside, New York 11377

The following are manufacturers and wholesale distributors of yarns and hooks:

American Thread Co
High Ridge Park
Stamford, Conn 06905
yarns

Boye Needles
The Newell Company
Freeport, Illinois 61032
hooks

Belding Lily Co
P O Box 88
Shelby, North Carolina 28150
novelty yarns

Reynolds Yarns, Inc
230 Fifth Avenue
New York, NY 10001
novelty yarns

Emile Bernat & Sons, Inc
230 Fifth Avenue
New York, NY 10001
yarns and hooks

William Unger & Co, Inc
230 Fifth Avenue
New York, NY 10001
novelty yarns

INDEX

Note: page numbers in *italics* refer to illustrations.

Acknowledgments

The publishers are very grateful to the following for kindly lending work to be photographed:

James Walters and Sylvia Cosh:
Solomon's knot curtain 39, beach bolero 38, woodland waistcoat and mohair cardigan 55.
Amanda Cosh: Amanda's mushrooms 39.
Muriel Kent: Tunisian jacket 54.
Gisela Banbury: handkerchief border 58.
José Butler: Victorian handkerchief bag 58.
Nancy Palmer-Jones: Jacquard top 63.
Heather Lickley: mohair bed-jacket 62.
Kathleen Basford: seamless jacket 66, oversweater 74.

Illustrations by Studio Briggs
Illustrations by Lucy Su on pages 1, 48, 56, 69

The following companies kindly lent items used in photography:

Dickens & Jones (straw beach hat – page 38, skirts and blouses – pages 54–55, 63); Fenwicks (skirts and blouses – pages 54–55, nightdress – page 62, clothes and accessories – pages 66–67); Graham & Green, 7 Elgin Crescent, London W11 (ivory frame – page 58); Laura Ashley, Sloane Street, London SW3 (child's dress and blouse – page 36, child's dress – page 42, white blouses – page 46, pinafore dress – pages 50–51); Nick Nacks, Wardour Street, London W1 (trousers and shirt – pages 74–75); Olof Daughters, Wigmore Street, London W1 (clogs – pages 39, 46); Ries Wools, 242/243 High Holborn, London WC1 (crochet hooks – pages 10–11)

Photography by : Theo Bergström endpapers; Camera Press 42, 43, 47, 50, 70, 70–1, 71; Oliver Hatch 6, 7, 10–11, 14–15, 18–19, 22–3, 26–7, 30, 31, 34, 35, 39 inset; Sandra Lousada 38, 39, 42, 46, 50–1, 51, 54, 55, 62, 63, 66, 66–7, 74–5; Spike Powell 2–3, 58–9.